A Vegetarians ecstasy

A Healthy Gourmet Celebration of over 250 no cholesterol, no dairy, lowfat recipes devoted to long life and good taste

James Levin, M.D. and Natalie Cederquist

Illustrations by
Natalie Cederquist

Published by
GLO, INC.

Revised Edition

Published by

Worldwide distribution by GLO, INC.

For information address:
GLO, Inc., 2406 Fifth Avenue, San Diego, CA 92101
U.S.A. and Canada call 1-800-854-2587 toll free
All other countries call 1-619-233-9165

Printed and bound in U.S.A.

Printed on Recycled Paper with Soya-based Inks

Library of Congress Catalog Card Number 90-86040
ISBN 0-9628698-7-2

14   13   12   11   10   9   8   7

This cookbook is dedicated to the ultimate health of all people. We inhabit this divine body, it is a gift, so please take care of it and of each other. Eating fresh, wholesome, light and alive foods will fill you full of their vitality and enable you to feel better than ever before. As each cell dances in celebration of the Universal vibration, you too will radiate this inner clarity of love.

Table of Contents

Foreword

A *Vegetarians Ecstasy* is a book for everyone, designed to show us how a high fiber, fresh fruit and vegetable diet with minimal fat can be divinely delicious.

The recipes contained herein include those from the exotic Pacific Rim to the sensual soulfood of Mexico and South America. Each recipe has easy to read large type and instructions for simple step by step preparation. The magical and inspired illustrations found throughout this book awaken one's visual appetite as well.

Most cookbooks (even vegetarian) call for too much fat, in the form of butter, dairy products, eggs, and other animal products.

We don't need all that fat!

We have spent several years improvising and substituting fresh herbs, lemon juice, cooking wines, soy products, tamari and vegetable broth to create a low fat tasty cuisine that is health promoting. We can sauté without butter or oil and still have our food taste great.

For the health and survival of our planet Earth and for our own personal health, it is time to learn a new way of eating; one that is environmentally clean and efficient, utilizing the dynamic variety of fresh produce, grains, beans, herbs and spices available.

This new way of eating is *A Vegetarians Ecstasy!*

Introduction

A special feast awaits you inside *A Vegetarians Ecstasy*. Over 250 healthful recipes have been prepared dedicated to long life and good taste.

Our vision is to present an ethnic variety of light sauces, salads, main dishes and desserts that elevate you into higher culinary consciousness.

Going beyond mere recipes we hope to encourage you towards the foods that give you more energy and vitality. The phrase "you are what you eat" is true on many levels, for health isn't just a diet but a way of life affected by what we eat, our state of mind, and our relationships. Real health involves the whole person, body, mind and soul.

Whole natural food brings to us a greater radiance and inner health. We consume the ultimate nutrition and energy when we eat raw and sprouted foods. Cooking destroys many of the vitamins and minerals of vegetables and fruits, so if possible, have a raw salad and plenty of fresh fruit, everyday. Begin substituting whole grains (wheat berries, brown rice, etc.) for refined flour products (breads, muffins, pastry). Whole grains provide the roughage and nutrition you need, balance your blood sugar levels, and contain less fat.

It takes more than healthy eating to maintain optimum health, for health is also a state of mind. Our mental pictures are the videotape for our physical well being. Visualize health, love, joy, peace, success and beauty and you will attract those things in your life. You are God's creation, what you create in your life is your gift in return.

By exercising and expending energy, you will gain energy. That is why a daily physical workout (whether walking, biking, swimming or dancing) is important for increasing your vitality and vigor, and will keep you looking and feeling younger. Also, surround yourself with positive people. The more loving, supportive, and harmonious our environment, the more conducive it is to experiencing a fuller healthier more vibrant life.

We see food not only as nourishment, but as a celebration of life. Be thankful for what you have, let love flow into your meal preparation and remember, real flavor comes from the heart.

May this book inspire your journey into lighter healthier eating.

Enjoy,
Natalie Cederquist
James Levin, M.D.

Buy Organic!

Did you know that the cell of an organically grown fruit or vegetable has a more vibrant and radiant life force than a cell smothered in chemical fertilizers and pesticides? One can certainly taste the difference. The organic one is tastier, sweeter and more potent than the commercial variety.

As we read about the effects pesticides have on our bodies, why take a chance?

Discover where to find organic produce in your area. By making the choice to shop organic you are supporting the organic farmers, and creating demand for a pesticide-free farm industry, which will lower the prices for organic produce. You will also consume a more nutritious product, rather than one depleted of its vitamins, minerals and trace elements from the leeching of toxic chemicals.

Growing your own seasonal vegetables and herbs is worth the effort. Try planting tomatoes in a 5 gallon tub, or herbs in a window box. One prolific zucchini plant should yield a summer supply of tender zucchinis. Planting also has a positive effect on our well-being.

If you can't buy organic then scrub or peel the produce or soak it in a vinegar bath several minutes before food preparation.

Just add 1 tbl. of white vinegar to a sinkful of cool filtered water, it will help rinse away some of the toxic residues.

And always send love into your meal by being thankful for what you are given.

Fats & Oils

Why not to heat them

Fatty acids, the building blocks of the fats in human bodies are a major energy source and important for the maintenance and construction of healthy cells. **Essential Fatty Acids** are called "essential" because our body doesn't manufacture them. Fresh raw seeds (especially flax seeds, see "Healing Heroes!"), nuts and oils are the healthiest sources of these fatty acids. When these natural and easily absorbed oils are heated above 320°F (160°c), their molecular structure transforms becoming harmful to our system, causing cellular degeneration.[1]

The process of hydrogenation turns liquid oil into hardened oil (shortenings and margarines) which destroys the Essential Fatty Acids (EFA's).

These adulterated fats don't belong in our bodies precise architectural plan. They become blocks to the natural life energy flow from cell to cell and impede the body's ability to absorb EFA's. They also may encourage fatty deposits in the liver (and other organs) and arteries. Fatty deposits in the arteries may lead to atherosclerosis. When our arteries are blocked the oxygen and blood can't flow to the heart and brain, so strokes and heart attacks are more likely to occur unless we clean up our diet.

For your health, it is best to avoid all products with hydrogenated and partially hydrogenated ingredients—read labels! In addition to margarine and shortening, hydrogenated products may be found in bakery goods, chips, crackers, fried foods and cereals. Some countries like Holland have banned the sale of margarines containing the altered fatty acids; interestingly, the Dutch are reported to have an average life expectancy 5 years longer than in the U.S.[2]

Oxidation and light also destroy the EFA's, therefore purchase oil in dark or metal containers, when possible.

Use only fresh, organic, mechanically pressed oil. Some good oils are walnut, safflower, olive, sesame, almond and flax. Avoid cottonseed oil, it is the most refined and pesticide contaminated oil.

Traditional frying overheats the oil (428°F), so take the care to use oil safely by *adding filtered water to the pan first.* In traditional chinese cooking, the water is put into a very hot wok, *then* the oil is added. The water will hold the temperature under 212°F, safe for the EFA's, and the waters vapor will guard against oxidation.

We prefer to use the sensitive oils, raw and uncooked for the most benefit in salad dressings or in the liver flush. For healthful cooking use lemon juice, sake or wine, liquid aminos or tamari to sauté your foods in. If desired, use a special oil (like toasted sesame oil) after cooking has been done.

You will preserve more than just the flavor, you will preserve your health.

How to Sauté without Oil

Heat 2-3 Tbl. of filtered water or vegetable broth in a heavy skillet. Add a bit of liquid aminos or tamari if you wish, and a splash of lemon juice, cooking wine, sake or a combination thereof. To enhance the taste of your vegetables, add your choice of the aromatics: minced ginger, garlic, onions, chile peppers or fresh herbs, and sauté on low heat for a couple of minutes. Next, add your chopped veggies, stirring them well to coat, sauté either covered or uncovered until al denté; season as desired. Cooking time depends on the size and quantity of the vegetables.

If you decide to use oil in your sauté, add filtered water to the pan first. The vapor will protect the oil from the heat, you'll use less fat, and you'll enjoy a healthier meal.

Glossary of Ingredients

Here is a guide to frequently used ingredients that might seem rather unusual at first. You can find all these foods in natural food stores or co-ops. These are vegetarian alternatives, supplements and staples. Stock and use these healthier substitutes instead of salt, cornstarch, eggs and meat, etc.

Agar Agar
A seaweed based thickener that gives a gelatinous body to foods. Especially good in fruit gels.

Arrowroot Powder
An herbal thickener, that when mixed with water into a paste thickens sauces and gravies; use instead of flour or cornstarch. Cornstarch creates a pasty glue-like coating over your intestines, and should be avoided.

Brewers and Nutritional Yeast
A potent vitamin, mineral, amino acid nutritive yeast that can be added to anything. It is one of the best sources of vitamin B-12. Add 1 Tbl daily to supplement your foods. Put it in your morning smoothies or atop a salad.

Egg Replacer
A potato starch and tapioca based flour, a leaven and binder that substitutes for egg yolks and whites. Use 1½ tsp. mixed with 2 Tbl water to replace 1 egg. One can also try tofu mashed with water as an egg replacer.

Liquid Aminos
A mineral rich soy bouillon developed by health pioneer Paul Bragg. It is a salt substitute with a distinctive delicious flavor to be used in sauces, dressings, salads, stir-frys and over vegetables. Use in a sauté along with water instead of oil and butter.

Mirin Cooking Sake

Mirin is the name of cooking sake. Sake is made from the action of a yeast-like mold on rice. It tenderizes and enhances your sautés and sauces, imparting natural sweetness.

Mirin has less alcohol than regular drinking sake. Look for it in Asian markets, or in the Oriental section of grocery stores.

Miso

An aged and fermented soy bean paste, high in B vitamins and enzymes. Thin with water, then add to soups and sauces during the last phase of cooking to keep all the nutrients alive. Miso provides a nice flavor and adds body to soups, sauces and gravies.

Seitan

A wheat gluten product that is found in the refrigerated section in natural food stores. Formed into a ball, seitan marinates in a savory sauce. You can slice it thin or cube it, marinate it with spices or barbeque it. Seitan was developed by Japanese warrior monks. It has a good meaty texture, and is high in protein and keeps in the refrigerator if it is well covered.

Seaweeds

Raised and bathed in the ocean, sea vegetables are charged with minerals, iodine, vitamins D, E, K, and B-complex, calcium and magnesium. They are healing to mucous membranes and skin irritations. There are many varieties: nori, wakame, hijiki, dulse, kombu. Rinse well several times before using, and add to salads or use as a condiment. Nutritious sea vegetables are a superior food, being so prolific they can be harvested daily to feed our planet.

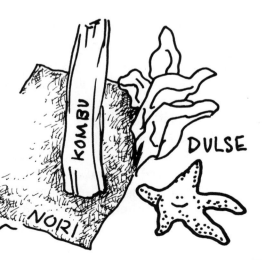

HIJIKI

KOMBU

DULSE

NORI

Tahini

Tahini has been used for over 3,000 years by the Egyptians and other cultures in the Middle East. This slightly bitter sesame butter thickens sauces, dressings and dips and is a great complement to rice and tofu. Mix with honey, maple syrup, bee pollen and dried fruit to create natural candies. Tahini is a good replacement for rich butter or dairy products.

Tamari

A naturally fermented soy bean sauce. Tamari is more concentrated than soy sauce; soy sauce is created from wheat and is a bit milder. Also, soy sauce usually contains sugar or preservatives, so be sure to search out the naturally brewed kind. Remember to dilute tamari with filtered water when using recipes calling for "soy sauce".

Tempeh

A staple and complete protein native to Indonesia. Soy beans are cooked, pressed into cakes and fermented. Steam, cook or marinate them first, then enjoy them with a myriad of sauces. Baked, broiled or barbequed, tempeh is a delicious meaty substitute high in B-12 and cholesterol free.

Tofu

Pressed soybean curd contains no cholesterol, and is a truly versatile protein food. Its uses are endless, from dips and drinks to main dishes and desserts. It comes in many varieties: soft, firm, silken and "Lite" (lowfat). Use the firm in stirfrys, and reserve the silken for blended sauces and desserts. Tofu has a neutral taste and it takes on whatever spice or seasoning you use with it. In summer months try serving it chilled and cubed in a bowl. Serve with separate seasonings such as minced green onions, tamari, ginger, and toasted sesame seeds.

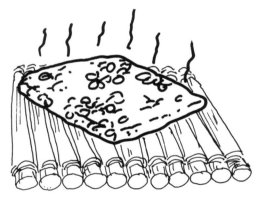

Exotic Mushrooms

There are several types of edible fungi (mushrooms) that are nutritious and considered a delicacy. Substitute them for white cap mushrooms to add variety and a new taste sensation to your meals.

All fresh mushrooms are wonderful in salads or stirfrys, and are preferred over canned varieties.

Enoki mushrooms are long, delicate and slender, resembling a sprout with a creamy colored small cap, use them whole.

Oyster mushrooms are large and flat, disc shaped and delicious.

Shiitake mushrooms are a large capped meaty mushroom, the thicker the better, great fresh or dried. Soak dried ones in warm filtered water for 20 minutes before stemming and adding to the wok.

Woodears are a rubbery fungus that have long been known in the East as a blood thinner. This beneficial anticoagulant keeps sticky platelets free flowing, here in the West we are just discovering its terrific qualities. Woodears yield little taste, but they add a lot of texture in woked dishes or salads.

Japanese Horseradish (Wasabi Powder)

Reconstitute wasabi in a small cup, mixing in a few drops of hot water to make a thick green paste. Its sharp flavor will ripen as it sits a few minutes; make only what you'll use for it will not keep. Its hot "bite" will clear your nasal passages effectively, and spice up sauces. Traditionally mixed with soy sauce to make a dipping sauce for sushi.

Enoki mushrooms

shiitake mushrooms

Dried Woodears

JAPANESE HORSE RADISH

Healing Heroes!

All raw fruits and vegetables are healing and nutritious, but there are some that are extraordinary. Here are a few of our favorites.

Have these wonder foods in stock at all times to cleanse, heal and protect your system against infection and environmental pollutants. Incorporate them into your daily regime for long life, good taste and vitality!

Garlic

Garlic is truly a blessed bulb, much revered for centuries for its medicinal properties. Its use in the remedy of 22 ailments was recorded in an Egyptian Medical listing, dated 1550 B.C. Garlic's healing qualities are also mentioned in a calendar of the Hsai dated 2000 B.C.[3]

Its anti-bacterial action is akin to penicillin and it has been used to treat high blood pressure, cardiac and circulatory problems, a wash for wounds and ulcers, a cure for worms and parasites, and for reducing cholesterol.

It eats away the skin (lipid layer) of harmful bacteria, preventing them from breathing, thus destroying them. Its healing power is released when the clove is crushed, evident by its powerful odor. Its beneficial properties are unstable in heat, so use garlic raw as much as possible. To retain the healing properties and fullest flavor, try stirring in pressed garlic after sauce has finished cooking.

For an easy way to peel a clove of garlic, hit the top with the flat side of a knife, or with the bottom of a mug. This will loosen the outer skin making it easy to peel off before chopping or pressing the garlic clove.

Ginger

This wondrous aromatic rhizome is soothing to the digestive system, stimulating to the circulary system, dispels gas, and works as a decongestant. It has been honored in ancient India and China and truly has an exotic taste.

Use it raw in dressings, soups, sauces and breads. As a tea, pour boiling water over chopped ginger for a warming effect when feeling chilled. Ginger is used in the Orange Flush.*

Lemon

A fantastic cleanser! It aids digestion, decongests, cleanses and stimulates the liver, it is a tonic to the heart and stomach and purifies the blood stream.

For extra strengthening to the liver add grated lemon peel to your raw salad. Each morning on an empty stomach take 1/2 lemon juiced in warm filtered water to cleanse your system and rid yourself of excess mucus—a great way to begin your day.

Flax

Its name derived from Latin means *most useful* and that it is. One of the oldest cultivated plants in history, flax is not only nutritious, but it is believed to be helpful in preventing disease and infection.

Flax has been of service to humanity prior to recorded history. Flax seeds and fiber cloth (linen) were found in archeological digs of ancient Babylonia, Egyptian burial chambers and Europe's stoneage ancestors, dating as far back as 5,000 B.C.

See page 34.

The oil in flax seed is the richest source of the Essential Fatty Acids LNA (linolenic acid) and LA (linoleic acid). "Essential" because the body cannot produce them. They are necessary for healthy nerves, arteries, blood, and vital to all cell walls. Flax regulates blood pressure and aids in the digestion and elimination of toxins due to its high mucilage and fiber content. It is a complete and easily digested protein, as well as an excellent vitamin and mineral source.

Good fresh Flax oil, due to its 3-month shelf life and extreme sensitivity to light, is available in health food stores. (Barlean's Oils)

To add Flax to your diet, try grinding it fresh minutes before use, or try the gomasio listed in the condiment section. Use it on salads, in your cereal, casseroles and smoothies, or just chew on a few seeds throughout the day.

Carrots

Carrots are good for increasing vitality, and the fresh raw juice is good for normalizing the entire system. Carrots aid in digestion, help to build blood, improve and maintain the bone structure and have been known to heal and prevent eye, throat, sinus and respiratory infections. Carrots are high in beta carotene (which helps the liver to isolate vitamin A).

Carrot juice is the richest source of vitamin A that the body can quickly assimilate. Fresh carrot juice also contains ample amounts of vitamins B, C, D, E, G and K.[4]

Carrot juice helps the liver to eliminate toxins via the lymph system and skin pores, thus if your skin turns an orange-like color it is due to this internal cleansing and is not caused from the orange color (or carotene) of carrot juice. Otherwise we would turn red from beets or turn green from broccoli. Live raw juices are truly terrific builders of health, they contain many enzymes and nutrients. If you are in need of a cleansing, fresh carrot juice may be used in a purifying fast.

Sprouts

The most alive foods on Earth are sprouts, for they are still growing at the table. Their protein, vitamin and mineral content rivals and surpasses almost any food. Sprouts are *biogenic*, full of vital life forces which build, cleanse, repair and strengthen our cells.

Awaken this life force by soaking the seeds or beans overnight in a glass jar filled with filtered water. This soaking activates the enzymes in the seeds which convert their starches into simple sugars, changes their complex fats into useable carbohydrates, and balances and predigests their proteins into an easily assimilated low calorie food source for just pennies.

The moisture content of sprouts also increases from about 10% to 88%, which is compositionally similar to any fruit, and to our own bodies.

Sprouts can be grown anywhere, anytime in just 3-7 days, they are your indoor organic garden.

Try sprouting lentils, alfalfa or mung beans to start, they are the easiest to sprout.

Simple Sprouting
1) Use 1/4c lentils, or mung beans, or 2 Tbl. alfalfa seeds per quart size glass jar.
2) Cover with pure water for 8-12 hours.
3) Rinse and drain 2 times daily (morning and night).
4) Put in sunlight for greenery to appear. Use either a screen or cheesecloth as a strainer for the top of the jar.

Beet & Carrot Greens
Create tender gourmet greens for your salads by placing the tops of these roots in a shallow pan of filtered water for a few days. Cut off greens as they grow.

Other Power Foods

Ginseng

The ancient Chinese health tonic for long life and enhanced physical performance is ginseng. The root is now harvested in the U.S. and is available in capsules, concentrates, teas and soft drinks. We enjoy it in liquid form added to juices and teas. In China they prescribe it for everything, especially for male vitality and increased energy.

Bee Pollen, Royal Jelly and Propolis

Pollen is one of the richest sources of vitamins, minerals, enzymes, fats, hormones, protein and amino acids. It has restorative properties for the entire system. One to three teaspoons is said to improve health, athletic performance and physical endurance. It is one of natures precious power foods, resembling multi-colored golden nuggets.

Royal bee jelly is secreted by the Queen Bee to feed other potential Royal Queen Bees. It is high in B vitamins and pantothenic acid, a cellular rejuvenator and energy-enhancer, it is also an excellent tonic for the heart.

The resinous substance gathered by the bees that is used to maintain and disinfect their hives is propolis. It is high in B complex vitamins and amino acids. Its natural antibiotic effect is said to heal wounds, ulcers, sore throats, oral infections and coughs. Look for the propolis lozenges and cough syrups now available in health food stores.

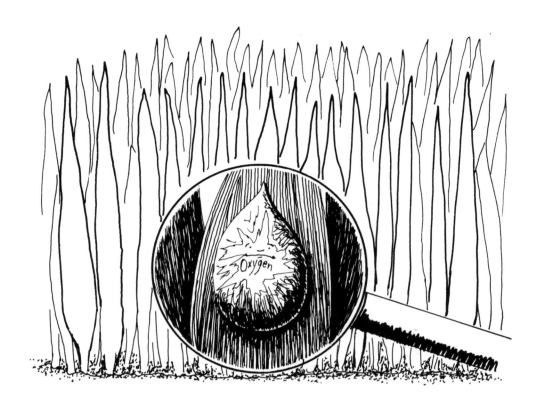

Wheatgrass Juice

Imagine drinking concentrated emeralds, liquid sweet and potent, healing and rejuvenating every cell of your body . . . welcome to wheatgrass juice! It is a complete food that detoxifies as it nourishes. Dr. G. H. Earp-Thomas, scientist and soil expert, has isolated over 100 elements and all the known minerals contained in wheatgrass. It contains almost the identical molecular makeup as the hemoglobin molecule of human blood, the difference is magnesium instead of iron. It oxygenates your system and it helps to build blood cells. It is said to produce an immunization effect against carcinogens, and to offset the effects of smog and environmental pollutants, x-rays and radiation. Truly this is a wonder food! If you don't grow wheatgrass, or have a juicer for that purpose, then call around to your local health food stores or juice bars to find out where you can get it freshly pressed. One ounce daily is sufficient, you can dilute it with water or fresh vegetable juice if desired. It is a healing wash for skin disorders and may be diluted for eye washes. Wheatgrass juice is such a powerful cleanser that you might have a few discomforts at first, but with continued usage it will detoxify your body and strengthen your entire system. Other chlorophyll rich supplements worth trying are bluegreen algae, spirulina and barley grass juice, they all share similar astounding health building properties.

Chiles

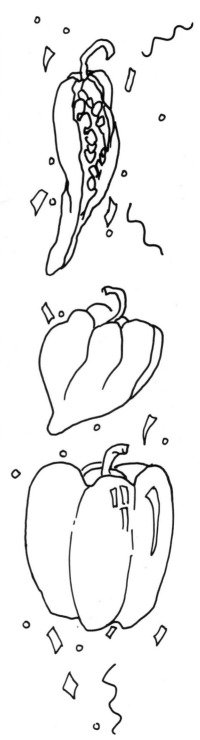

Chiles are a passion in the heart of Mexican and Indian cuisines. They are also gaining respect as a versatile vegetable and seasoning in nouvelle cooking. Chiles are loaded with vitamin C, high in iron, potassium and niacin. The niacin in chiles improves circulation, reduces cholesterol levels in the blood, and is said to protect cells against cancer.

Chiles are an effective guard against colds. They are fantastic stuffed, baked, roasted, minced or raw, and the hot ones are indispensable in salsas.

There are many kinds of peppers in the Chile (capsicum) family, here is a brief description of the most common ones.

Ancho or pasilla chiles

These chiles are rather heart shaped and are not as hot as the anaheim. The dried version is quite dark and wrinkly. The pulp is a classic for enchilada sauces, yielding a sweet and roasted flavor. Note: if the cooked pulp is black or dark brown it will make the sauce rather smokey flavored and bitter tasting.

Bell Peppers

The most familiar and versatile chiles are green peppers. When allowed to ripen on the vine they turn yellow then red, increasing in sweetness and nutrition.

California (anaheim) Chiles

Longer, thinner and hotter than the bell pepper, the anaheim chile can be roasted and peeled, stuffed and baked, or minced raw before adding to soups, sauces or main dishes.

The seeds are hot, as with all chiles so discard before use or use with caution. As these chiles dry to a brick red color they become hotter. The cooked pulp is a natural thickener and adds an authentic flavor to sauces. Hanging chile clusters in your kitchen enables you to pull one off when you need one and adds a colorful ethnic adornment.

Jalapeños

Plump green peppers about 2" in length. Raw, minced, sliced or roasted they are excellent in many sauce or main dish creations. They are hotter than the Ancho chiles.

Serranos

A small slender hot green pepper that can really spice up a soup or sauce. Frequently found floating in Thai soups for flavor, they are meant to be strained out. These can really make your eyes water, so be careful.

Cayenne Pepper

A favorite seasoning. Gives an invigorating warming effect by increasing circulation, which is beneficial to the heart and the blood stream. Try it in water with lemon juice as a daily tonic.

How to Roast a Chile

1) Preheat oven to 450°.
2) Rinse chile, blot dry, put them on the top rack in the oven.
3) Turn chiles after a few minutes so the skin blisters evenly.
4) Pull out chiles and put them into a plastic bag until cool, or rinse in cool water. Peel off skin, dig out seeds, keep stem on only if stuffing them.
5) Chop chiles and add to your creations, or keep the chile whole to make *Chiles Rellenos*, or other stuffed *exóticas*.

How to Handle a Chile

Wear rubber gloves! Or, wash your hands with soap and water before touching *anything* else.

Let's hear it for the bean....

Soy Products

Dairyless and Eggless

With optimum health in mind, we have chosen to use soy products and egg replacer rather than dairy and eggs. Dairy is mucus forming, it contains cholesterol, fat and hormones, in addition to the pesticides and antibiotics used in the farming and dairy industry.

Soy and seed cheeses, soy yogurts, soy milks and almond milks, soy and rice based ice creams are delicious non-dairy products in the natural markets for you to try which are cholesterol free and low in fat.

BEGINNINGS

♥ Fat Free
* Use fat free soy milk

HEALTHY BEGINNINGS
Breakfast Ecstasies

Upon arising, it is beneficial to awaken your system with warm water and lemon juice. This drink purifies your system (especially the liver) and flushes out impurities.

Follow this cleansing with the Orange Flush, then have herbal tea, or fresh juice of choice. We find that exercise is fantastic at this point, before eating solid foods. It will help you to wake up your system by flooding oxygen into your blood stream, circulating energy throughout your body and preparing you for a healthy assimilation of food. Have a good aerobic workout (minimum of 20 minutes) before breakfast.

The best break-fast we know is a bowl of fresh cut fruit. For a nourishing light meal make a fruit smoothie, they fill you up, are easy to digest, and are low in fat and calories. Try adding fresh or frozen fruit, soy-based protein powder, bee pollen, brewers yeast, tofu, bran or spirulina to fresh juice for a delicious meal. Complement it with a muffin for a super morning filler. You can make these muffins in advance, freeze them, and reheat in an oven when you want.

Any cooked whole grain makes a nourishing first meal, too. Try whole oats, rye flakes or müesli. Special brunch dishes like Tofu Rancheros, Tofu Florentine or Tofu Chilaquiles create celebrative weekend meals without oil, dairy or eggs.

Lemon Water

The morning cleanser

Begin your day with a cup of warm filtered water with 1/2 a lemon juiced into it. You can also substitute 1/2 tsp of raw apple cider vinegar. This restores the acidic balance in your body, and is a very cleansing and purifying way to start your day.

Lemon juice flushes out impurities and excess mucus, cleanses the liver and acts as a natural appetite suppressant. Wait 15 to 30 minutes before consuming other beverages or foods, so the lemon has a chance to do its magic.

THE Orange Flush

This Liver flush was designed by Dr. Stone and has super cleansing, strengthening and invigorating properties for your liver and whole system in general. You can moderate the garlic and cayenne according to taste. The Purifying Diet by Dr. Stone is a wonderfully gentle way to heal and cleanse. It consists of this flush every morning and eating *only* fruits and vegetables, (raw or steamed) plus herbal teas throughout the day.

2 c	Fresh squeezed orange/grapefruit juice
1/2	Lemon juiced
1 tsp	olive oil—extra virgin pure (or flax seed oil)
1 tsp	Fresh ginger, skinned and chopped
1	garlic clove, chopped
dash of	cayenne

Blend everything in a blender; first on low, then on high until frothy. Strain into goblets. This drink can be moderated by omitting the lemon juice.

Master Cleanser

This was developed by Stanley Burroughs and is a great way to fast, drinking at least 1 gallon of Master Cleanser a day.

1/4 c	Lemon juice
1/4 c	Maple syrup
1/2 tsp	Cayenne
1 qrt	Filtered water (pure)

Mix all of the ingredients together. The lemon acts as a purifier and toner, the cayenne increases circulation and the maple syrup supplies the necessary glucose to maintain your energy.

ALSO...

In between meals:
Carry with you a 1/2 gallon bottle or thermos full of purified water with the juice of a few lemons. It will cleanse your system, keep you hydrated, and ward off hunger.

ꙮ Gorilla Juice ꙮ

A high energy, nonfat, after/workout fortifier. The green color is due to the chlorophyll. Isn't it amazing that the Gorilla's awesome strength and gentle nature come from a diet of only raw fruits and vegetables!

Per person:

2 c	**Filtered water** (for a sweet version use 1 cup filtered water and 1 cup pineapple juice)
1 tsp	**Spirulina powder**
	Dash of Cayenne pepper
1 Tbl	**Lemon juice**

Blend well and serve on ice, or chilled.

Sweet Rice Tea

A healthy version of Mexican "horchata." Soaking rice overnight breaks down the starch, making a nourishing chilled drink on hot days, or to accompany hot foods. For a creamier tea, substitute Vanilla Lite soymilk for 1/2 of the filtered water.

1 c	**Organic brown rice, well rinsed**
1½ qrt	**Filtered water, with 1/4 c lemon juice squeezed in**
1/3 c	**Honey or maple syrup**
1 tsp	**Cinnamon**
1/2 tsp each	**Cardamon and grated orange peel**
1	**Organic orange, seeded and sliced**

1) Soak the rice in 1/2 of the filtered water overnight (8-12 hours), in a glass jar or ceramic container. Rinse and strain.
2) Blend the rice with the filtered water, strain into a pitcher.
3) Add the spices, filtered water and honey to the rice. Serve on ice, float an orange slice in each glass.

Serves 4

Enlightn' Mint Tea

Fresh squeezed citrus goes well with mint tea, serve chilled or on ice.

6	Mint tea bags (about 4 Tbl loose tea)
1 qrt	Filtered water
2	Oranges, juiced (about 3/4 c)
1	Lemon, juiced (about 1/4 c)
2 Tbl	Honey

Sun tea method: Add the tea bags to the filtered water in a glass jar—let the jar sit in the sun for 5 hours or longer. Remove the tea bags, then add the rest of the ingredients and chill.

Stove method: Steep the tea bags in a cup of boiling water for 10 minutes. Remove the tea bags, stir in the honey, pour (or strain) into a pitcher, add the rest of the water and juices—chill.

Makes 6 cups

Hibiscus Cooler

A hot weather tropical drink with a pretty ruby red color.

1/2 c	Hibiscus flowers (dried herb)
1/4 c	Rose hips (dried)
1½ qrt	Filtered water
1 c each	Orange juice and pineapple juice
1/4 c	Lemon juice
1/4 c	Honey

1) Cover the herbs with 2 cups of boiling filtered water, cover and let sit for 15 minutes, stir in the honey and strain the liquid into a pitcher.
2) Stir in the rest of the ingredients, chill and serve on ice.

Garnish with a pineapple wedge or orange slice if desired.
Makes 8½ cups.

Easy Nut Milks

Soaking releases and increases the nutrients in nuts making them a more digestible protein, Nut milks also make a healthy alternative to cow's milk. Makes 3½ cups.

> 1/2 c   **Almonds or cashews**
> 3 c   **Filtered water**
> **(you can add dried fruit to the soak water too: apricots, raisins, dates, etc.)**

1) Soak the nuts together in the filtered water to cover overnight. Rinse and drain.
2) Blend the rice and filtered water in a blender until creamy (several minutes).
3) Sweeten to taste with honey, barley malt or maple syrup. Strain and serve on ice, or serve hot on a cold night with added cinnamon, cardamon, nutmeg and vanilla.

Carob Almond Mild

Follow directions above using almonds.

Adding
> 2 Tbl   **Honey or maple syrup**
> 1 tsp   **Carob powder**
> 1/2 tsp   **Vanilla**

Strain, chill or serve warm with an extra cup of soymilk added if you desire.

For smoothies
Blend the nut milk with frozen bananas (and vegetable protein powder) for a truly delicious shake.

Try these combinations
Almond Apricot with cardamon and nutmeg
Cashew Date with cinnamon
Cashew Banana (Blend a Banana in for extra potassium)

DRINKS & SMOOTHIES

Instead of eating a meal, try drinking your breakfast & lunch.

Tofu Nanaphant

2 oz	Tofu
1 c	Apple juice
1	Banana
	Cracked ice
1 tsp	Peanut butter
1 Tbl	Lemon juice

Froggy's Quantum Leap

1 tsp	Spirulina
1½ c	Orange juice
1	Frozen chopped banana

Protein Berry

1/2 c	Frozen berries of your choice
1½ c	Juice or soy milk
2 Tbl	Protein powder (soy-based)

Humming Birds' Buzzzz

1 Tbl	Bee pollen
1/2 c	Frozen raspberries or strawberries
1½ c	Cherry cider or cran/raspberry juice

Power Fruit Smoothie

1 Tbl	Protein powder
1/2 c	Vanilla soy milk
1 c	Orange juice
1	Banana
5	Frozen strawberries
1/4	Apple

Put all of the ingredients into a blender and blend well. 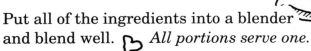 *All portions serve one.*

Sunday Scrambler

A yummy brunch star with no cholesterol.

1 Tbl	Liquid aminos (see page 14)
2 Tbl	Filtered water
1	Garlic clove, pressed
1/2	Onion, sliced
1 c	Tofu
a dash of	Turmeric
1 drop	Toasted sesame oil
1	Tomato, cut into wedges or seeded and chopped

1) Heat the liquid aminos and filtered water in a wok or skillet, add the garlic, stir quickly.
2) Add the onions and spices, saute briefly until tender.
3) Add the tofu, simmer 5 minutes.
4) Toss in the tomato wedges 1 minute before serving.

Serves 2

Tofu Florentine

*Sautéed tofu nestles on a bed of sautéed spinach topped with
a **Light Lemon Sauce**. A light version of Eggs Florentine.*

Per person:

2 oz	Tofu (1/2" thick cutlet)
1 tsp each	Liquid aminos, lemon juice, filtered water
2 c	Spinach leaves, packed fresh (or about 10 oz. frozen)
1/4 c	Light Lemon Sauce (p. 134), warmed
1 Tbl	Wine
	Fresh nutmeg and black pepper

1) Sauté the tofu in liquids (not wine) in a small skillet,
   sprinkle on spices. Cook both sides—set the tofu aside on
   another plate.
2) Add spinach leaves and wine to the skillet, stir quickly over
   a medium high heat—only 3-4 minutes.
3) Make a bed of spinach on each plate, place the tofu filet on
   top. Drizzle sauce on top. Garnish with a lemon butterfly
   (see page 61).

Tofu Rancheros

An egg-less, oil-less version of Huevos (eggs) Rancheros.
This country style dish layers a tortilla, tofu, and chile sauce
and tops it with soy cheese, onions, peppers or whatever you wish.
Serve with rice and beans, or fresh fruit for a hearty brunch.
Make the sauce ahead for a quick morning preparation.

Per person:

1	**Corn tortilla**
2 oz	**Firm tofu (1/2" thick cutlet)**
1 tsp	**Liquid aminos**
1 tsp	**Filtered water**
1/4 c	**Red onions, sliced**
1/4 c	**Chile Roja Enchilada Sauce* (p. 129), warmed**
1/4 c	**Soy cheese, grated**
	Garnish of choice: peppers, green onions, avocados, black olives, sprouts, etc.

1) Toast the tortilla until crisp, but not browned.
2) Sauté the tofu in the liquid aminos and water in a skillet, cook both sides. Add the onions, and stir for 2 minutes more. Set aside onto a dish.
3) Put the crisp tortilla into the skillet, arrange the tofu on top, pour the sauce on top, and add soy cheese. Cover and turn to low, cook until the soy cheese melts (just a couple of minutes).
4) Slide onto a plate and garnish.

** You can also serve this with **Meximato sauce** (page 142).*

Tofu Chilaquiles

(Cheelah-kee-less)

An intoxicating way to use up leftover tortillas. Delicious for Sunday Brunch or lighter meals.

1/2 dz	Corn tortillas
1/2 lb	Firm tofu
1 Tbl	Liquid aminos
1/2 Tbl	Filtered water
1/2 c	Onion, sliced
1/2 c	Salsa Verde or Chile Verde Sauce (p. 130)
1/2 c	Soy jack cheese

1) Halve the tortillas, then cut them into 1/2" strips. Cut tofu into 1/2" cubes. Toast the tortilla strips in the oven until slightly crisp.
2) Heat wok on high. Add the liquid aminos and the filtered water, then add the tortillas strips and sauté on high, stirring quickly until crisp and meaty.
3) Add the sliced onion and tofu, and continue stirring.
4) Add the soy cheese and stir in 1/4 cup of sauce. Then turn to low, heat for a few minutes.
5) Serve with heated sauce on top and a cilantro garnish.

*Serve with **Yucatan Fruit Salad** (page 63) and a sparkling juice beverage.*

Serves 2-3

Breakfast Apple Torte

This looks and tastes sensational.
For desert, try topping it with vanilla soy ice cream.

4 large	**Granny Smith apples, (or 8 Pippins)**
1 Tbl	**Egg replacer mixed with 4 Tbl filtered water**
3/4 c	**Vanilla soy milk**
3/4 c	**Whole wheat pastry flour**
1 tsp	**Vanilla**

Cinnamon and honey drizzled on top

1) Peel, core and thinly slice the apples—preheat the oven at 375°.
2) Beat the egg replacer with water, add soymilk and vanilla stir in flour.
3) Spray a baking dish or skillet with vegetable spray. Arrange the apples in a swirl pattern and pour the batter on top.
4) Swirl on the honey and cinnamon and bake at 350° for 25 min.

Serve 4-5

Morning Fruit Crisp

A quick breakfast treat using fresh fruit.

Per person:

1 c	**Peaches, apricots, pears, any fresh fruit in season**
1/4 c	**Granola of choice**
1 Tbl	**Natural fruit syrup**
	Soy milk

1) Slice your fruit of choice, then arrange it in a baking dish.
2) Sprinkle the granola on top, swirling a little syrup over it.
3) Bake at 350° for 20 min.
4) Serve in bowls with soymilk if desired.

Müesli

Prepare the night before or let sit an hour or two before serving.

Per person serving:

1 tsp	**Honey or apple concentrate**
1/2	**Apple, grated**
1/4 c	**Whole grain flakes (oat, rye, wheat or mixture)**
1 Tbl	**Ground flax seed**
1 Tbl	**Oatbran**
	Soaked raisins and almonds

Mix all together and let the mixture soak in either soy yogurt, apple juice or soymilk until grain flakes soften. Spice it as you like with cinnamon, vanilla or maple extract. Serve with fresh fruit on top.

The Universal Tofu Pancake

No eggs in this nourishing thin pancake,
delicately sweetened with banana.

1 pack	Silken "lite" tofu (10.5 oz.)
1/2 c	Vanilla soy milk
1 Tbl	Honey
1/2	Banana
1 c	Wholewheat pastry flour
1 Tbl	Baking powder
1 Tbl	Vegetable oil

1) Heat a non-stick griddle on medium heat for a couple minutes, then turn to low.
2) Blend the first 4 ingredients in a blender. Put the dry ingredients into a bowl and whisk in the wet blended ingredients. Let sit for a couple minutes.
3) Spray skillet with vegetable spray. Pour the batter on in 4" circles and heat until golden; when bubbles appear, flip and heat other side. Pancakes will flip easily if griddle is sufficiently preheated, and if pancake batter has cooked enough.
4) Serve with maple syrup, fruit syrup or fresh fruit and soy yogurt.

Vanilla Fruit Crepes

1 Recipe	Universal Tofu Pancake, as prepared above
	Soy vanilla yogurt, stirred well
	Fresh fruit or berries of choice (sliced peaches, apricots or strawberries are superb)

1) Spread the batter on a hot griddle making large circles as thin as possible.
2) Assemble: Put the soy yogurt and fruit inside or the soy yogurt inside and roll up with the fruit on top, either way tastes great!
3) Warm the stuffed crepes in the oven before serving or serve 'em as you make 'em.

Blue Corn Raspberry Muffins

Blue corn contains more nutrients than yellow corn.

1 c	Blue corn meal*
1 c	Whole wheat pastry flour
1 Tbl	Baking powder
1 Tbl	Soy protein powder
1 tsp	Cinnamon
1 c	Apple juice
1/2 c	Soft tofu
1/4 c	Honey
1 Tbl	Egg replacer
1/2 c	Walnuts, chopped
1 c	Fresh or frozen raspberries

1) Sift the first 5 ingredients into a medium bowl. Blend the next 4 items, and pour them into the bowl. Stir in the rest of the ingredients gently and spoon them into a lightly oiled muffin tin.
2) Bake at 375° for 30-35 minutes, makes 1 dozen.

* If you can't find blue corn meal, then use 2 cups of blue corn pancake mix and omit the pastry flour, reduce baking powder to 1/2 Tbl.

Zucchini Raisin Muffins

Delicate zucchinis make these muffins moist.

1/4 c	Raisins
1/2 c each	Bran and boiling filtered water
1/2 c	Orange juice
1/3 c	Honey
2 c	Shredded zucchinis
1 Tbl	Egg replacer mixed with 4 Tbl filtered water
1 c	Whole wheat pastry flour
1/2 c	Blue or yellow corn meal
4 tsp	Baking powder
2 tsp	Cinnamon

1) Let the raisins and the bran soak in the filtered water, preheat oven to 375°.
2) Stir together the orange juice, honey, zucchinis and egg replacer, then stir into the raisin bran mix.
3) Stir the dry ingredients separately, then fold them into the wet mixture.
4) Pour the batter into an oiled muffin tin and bake at 375° for 20 minutes.

Makes 12 muffins.

Layered Maple Oat Muffins

A delicious way to eat oat bran.
These make a wonderful breakfast treat.

1 c	Oat bran
3/4 c	"Lite" soy milk
1½ tsp	Egg replacer mixed with 2 Tbl filtered water
1/3 c	Applesauce
2	Ripe bananas
1 c	Unbleached or whole wheat pastry flour
2½ tsp	Baking soda
1 tsp	Baking powder
1/2 c	Maple syrup
1/2 c	Walnuts or almonds, ground
2 Tbl	Whole wheat pastry flour
1 tsp	Cinnamon

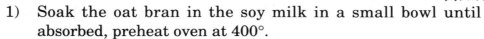

1) Soak the oat bran in the soy milk in a small bowl until absorbed, preheat oven at 400°.
2) Beat the egg replacer and water in a food processor until fluffy. Add the applesauce and bananas, beat well. Blend in the oat bran mixture.
3) In a separate bowl mix the flour with soda and baking powder, then add them to the above mixture until just barely mixed. Mix the last 4 items in a separate bowl.*
4) Lightly oil a muffin tin and fill it full with batter, then alternate with the maple filling until the muffin tin is full.
5) Bake at 375° for 20 minutes.

Makes 10 muffins.

*Add 1 tsp of maple extract for an enhanced maple flavor

Apple Oatbran Muffins

A moist and delicious muffin without eggs or oil,
producing a very light texture.

3 c	Oatbran (rice or wheat bran can substitute)
1 c	Boiling Filtered water
3 tsp	Egg replacer mixed with 4 Tbl filtered water
3/4 c	Rice syrup, barley malt syrup or honey
2 c	Vanilla "Lite" Soy Milk
1 c	Toasted black walnuts, chopped
2 c	Whole wheat pastry flour
1/2 tsp each	Cinnamon and clove powder
2½ tsp	Baking soda
2 c	Grated apple

1) Let the bran soak in the filtered water till absorbed, preheat oven at 375°.
2) Beat the egg replacer, honey, and soy milk together, then mix into the bran mixture. Stir in the apples and nuts.
3) Sift together the dry ingredients and then fold the dry mixture into the wet mixture.
4) Pour the batter into a lightly oiled muffin tin and bake at 375° for 25 minutes—Batter keeps in the refrigerator for several weeks (cover tightly).

Makes 16 muffins.

Pineapple Nut Oatbran Muffins ⋆

Follow recipe above and instead of apple add,

2 c	Chunk pineapple (instead of 2 c apple)
1/2 c	Date sugar instead of honey
	Delete clove powder

Also, macadamia nuts are a nice substitute for walnuts.

Müesli Muffins

Yields 1 dozen healthy, easy to prepare muffins.

Preheat oven at 400°

1 lb	**Tofu, soft**
1/2 c	**Orange juice, fresh**
2 Tbl	**Honey**
1/4 c	**Fructose**
1	**Banana, chopped**
1 tsp	**Vanilla**
1 Tbl	**Baking powder**
1 tsp	**Baking soda**
1 c	**Whole wheat pastry flour**
1¼ c	**Müesli (whole grain flakes with raisins)**

1) Blend the first six items in a blender or food processor.
2) In another bowl, sift the dry ingredients together.
3) Gently fold the dry ingredients into the wet, spoon batter into lightly oiled muffin tins and bake at 375° for 20 minutes, or until toothpick inserted comes out clean.

Makes 12 muffins

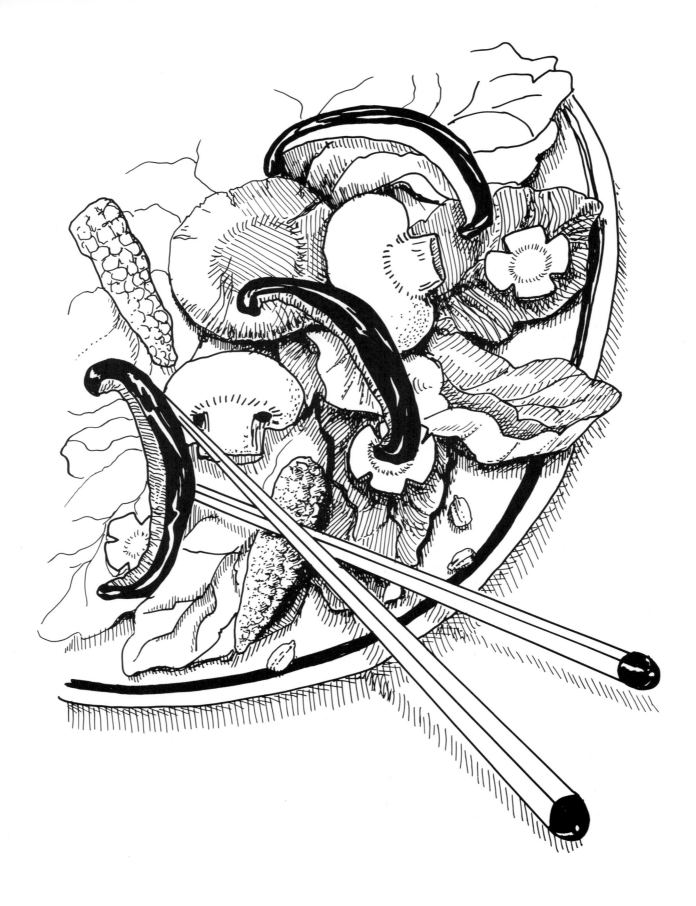

SALADS

♥ Fat Free

SALADS

Fruits and vegetables are some of the most abundant, nourishing and giving friends we have. They come to us in so many luscious and colorful varieties. They are best eaten right out of the garden or off the trees, so search out the farmers markets and organic grocers near you to enjoy the freshest, tastiest produce possible. Raw vegetables and fruits are so good for you. They are an abundant source of fiber, vitamins, minerals and enzymes. Try eating more fresh fruits and vegetables, substituting a crunchy raw carrot for chips and see the difference it makes: you'll feel lighter and brighter.

May these recipes spark your culinary creativity and send you on many tasty travels through the Garden of Eatin'.

Color, Texture & Flavor

The human spirit cannot be contained. As the walls dissolve that have separated the nations, we experience the synthesis of One Great Humanity. As we welcome our mighty multi-cultural world, we also welcome the dynamic variety of foods from around the globe. This endless exploration of new flavors, textures and colors enlivens and expands our senses, through preparing the traditional and in combining for the new. Be adventurous! Experiment with foods you've never tried, letting your imagination play in the great abundance of variety.

May the following ideas ignite your own culinary exploration of transforming ordinary foods into a work of art.

Here are some thoughts regarding the color, texture and flavor of food, as living sculptures of the Divine.

Color

The color of whole natural food, like all living things, is the expression of white light through the spectrum, each color transmitting an energy vibration. Color is a feast for the eyes; healing mind, body, and soul, as well as appetizing to the palate. Balance the colors in a meal, use red, orange, yellow, green, blue, purple and white for a visual delight. Eating foods according to their color is an aspect of the Rainbow Diet: relying upon the outer color or vibration of food to correspond to the chakras (energy centers) of the body[5].

For example, red foods, (red apples, strawberries, etc.) link to the base or lower chakra and energize the system. Green foods (green leafy plants and vegetables) promote calmness and are healing to the heart chakra. Blue foods (blueberries, blue corn, potatoes, grapes) link to the throat chakra and enhance our creativity[6]. Also try eating warm colored foods (red, orange and yellow) in the morning and cool colors later on in the day (green, blue and purple). Use white-gold foods (soy products, grains, papaya, etc.) with any meal.

Use complementary colors to enhance and excite your visual display of meals. From red, yellow, and blue, one can derive all colors. These are the primary colors. Mix primaries to create secondary colors: yellow and red create orange, red and blue create purple, blue and yellow create green. Have fun visually complementing foods with this easy way of determining color opposites:

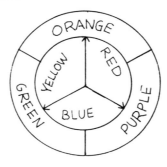

To discover the opposite complementary color of red tomatoes for example, mix the remaining two primaries (yellow and blue) to find green. Use green leaves, herbs or vegetables to visually complement red tomatoes. Yellow vegetables should be accented with something purple, like grated beets or red cabbage. Enliven an orange salad with blueberries.

Blue/orange, red/green, and purple/yellow themes produce electric and beautiful contrasts. Painters play off these opposites to create more vividness in their paintings, opposites vibrate each other and become more brilliant than if placed next to similar colors.

Colors truly are nourishing light rays, dynamically enhancing our daily life.

Texture

Texture is the surface arrangement of your food and is fun to vary. In one dish meals such as mandala salads, cut your vegetables in different ways. You can create a masterpiece by shredding one vegetable, cutting, tearing or mincing others. For special occasions try cutting a star or flower shape out of carrots, carve moons out of cucumbers, sliver zucchinis so long and fine that they resemble pasta. Combine the natural beauty of whole foods with the art of cutting. This is a zen approach to food presentation as in Ikeban, the Japanese Art of flower arranging. Work with nature to create inspiring edible art for the soul. (See "Culinary Decorations", page 61, for a guide to garnishes and cutting ideas.)

Flavors

A rich melody of tastes are created by combining different flavors. More attentive smelling will exalt and educate your taste buds, since taste and smell work in tandem. Balancing sweet, salty, sour and spicy is an art to learn through practice and tasting. Discover these alternatives: for **hot**; try cayenne pepper, horseradish, and all chiles fresh or dried. For **sweet**; there is honey, maple syrup, concentrated fruit juices, fresh and dried fruit, barley malt and rice syrup. **Salty** alternatives are liquid aminos, miso, umeboshi paste, tamari, sea salt, and Bronner's liquid soy bouillon. **Sour** is found in citrus (limes and lemons) and vinegars.

Pungent and **spicy** flavors are garlic, ginger, onion, curry powders, cumin, chiles and other dried spices.

To bring out the flavor of root vegetables (carrots, beets, turnips, radishes) and make them easier to digest when eaten raw, increase the surface area by finely grating them in the food processor.

Natural flavors are truly the best. Use herbs and spices to accent foods rather than fats and oils. Herbs are less fattening, cleaner and easier for your system to digest. Also experiment with the different flavors that wines bring to food. The quality of the wines essence will linger long after the evaporation of the alcohol.

By creating and experiencing new flavors and tastes in our food preparation, we awaken the full potential of our senses through the foods that we eat.

Cutting Techniques
A basic visual guide to common cuts.

Angled cuts
Hold knife at an angle pointed away from you, as you slice the vegetables.

Chop
Cut in uniform pieces, about 1/2" thick.

Coarse chop
Larger cuts, from about 1" thick.

Crush
Use a blender or coffee/nut grinder to pulverize whole seeds, pods, herbs and spices. Crushing spices prior to usage produces the freshest flavors and releases wonderful aromas in your kitchen.

Cube or dice
Small cube-shaped sections are made by slicing horizontally in 1/2" intervals, then slicing vertical at 1/2" intervals. Dicing is a smaller version of the cube.

Julienne
Cutting vegetables horizontally at 1/4" intervals, then cut lengthwise into match sticks. (Named after the French chef Julien in 1785.)

Mince
Finely dice using a large knife or cleaver, continue scraping food into a mound and chop until all pieces are a uniform 1/16"-1/8" size.

Slice
Cut into 1/4" wide sections.

Sliver
Cut into 1/16"-1/8" wide sections.

Shred
Use a grater or food processor to shear thin sections off carrots, cabbage or beets, making them easier to eat raw in salad form.

Culinary Decorations

A garnish can be as simple as a parsley spig, or as complex as carving a swan out of a block of ice. There are many ways to transform your meal into a work of art with little effort.

Here are a few fun ways to create new shapes out of ordinary foods. Wash your produce before beginning and use sharp utensils.

Radish UFO's
Slice radish into disks, cut a slice halfway through, fit two sliced edges together, like two intersecting planes.

Zucchini Flowers
Slice zucchini lengthwise into 1/8" thickness, then cut small slices along one edge—creating a "comb" effect. Twirl it around, spiraling it from the outside in, to make a flower shape. Lay a red grape in the center.

Lemon lime butterflies
Slice thinly and cut triangles or 1/2 moons out of citrus. Place 2 edges together and use a thin chive or red pepper strip as antennae.

Chile Flowers
Slice lengthwise into strips leaving stems attached, shake out seeds. Put in ice water until tips curl out.

Rose buds
Trim bottom off radishes so they can sit flat. Slice 4-5 petals around radish perimeter. Pare center into an oval. Chill in ice water until petals open. Make large roses from turnips by cutting petals all around perimeter.

Carrot ribbons

Peel carrot and use a paring knife to peel off thick peels or "ribbons". Roll each peel up into a curl and place into a small ice cube tray. Put in freezer for an hour, then unwind and twist ribbons onto plates.

Leek laces

Cook leek leaves until tender. Cut into 6-7" lengths and place on plates. Place steamed asparagus, carrot or yellow squash strips on top and tie leek laces around them creating a bundle.

Pepper triangles

Use red, yellow or green pepper sections (2"x3" flat shape) to create fun triangles. Make 1 cut halfway up pepper on opposing sides, twist and pull apart into a triangle shape.

Carrot sticks and flowers

Cut 4 "V" shapes lengthwise down carrot—a 4-petaled "flower" will be left after you make thin slices across carrot.

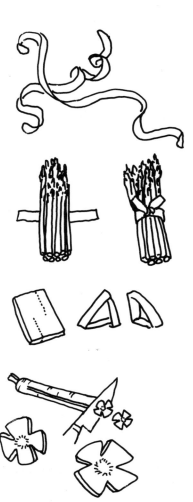

Yucatan Fruit Salad

A superb complement to Mexican main dishes (i.e., enchiladas, rellenos)
this is the first course to be devoured.

2 c	**Fresh pineapple**
1 sm	**Jicama**
1 lg	**Mango (not too soft)**
1 tsp	**Jalapeño pepper, chopped**
2 Tbl	**Packed cilantro leaves**
1	**Lime, juiced**
1 tsp	**Poppy seeds**

1) Chop the pineapple, jicama and mango, put them into a bowl.
2) Put the jalapeño chunks through a garlic press and press their juice onto the fruit, discard the fibers inside the press.
3) Chop the cilantro leaves and add with rest of spices.

Chill.

Hawaiian Pineapple Boats

The pineapple shell becomes the serving bowl in this pretty party salad.

1 lg	**Pineapple**
3	**Bananas**
3	**Kiwis**
18	**Strawberries**

1) Slice the pineapple lengthwise, cut the core out of each half. Cut the pineapple out into chunks. Set aside in a medium bowl.
2) Slice the rest of the fruit, add fruit to the bowl with the pineapple.
3) Fill the pineapple halves and decorate with long spears from the pineapple cores, or you can cut the cores into shapes and hold them with toothpicks.

Papaya Kiwi Salad

*A refreshing and delightful salad that also makes a great light dessert,
excellent for digestion.*

1	**Papaya (or half a Mexican papaya)**
1-2	**Kiwis**
1/4 c	**Raisins**
1	**Lime, cut in half (juice one half, quarter other half)**

1) Peel and slice the papaya into small spears, peel and quarter the kiwis.
2) Arrange the papaya and kiwi on a beautiful platter and sprinkle with raisins and lime juice.

Serve 1/2 the lime in wedges on the side.

Serves 2-4

Independence Day Salad

A Red, White & Blue Salad

1 basket	**Strawberries**
2	**Bananas**
1/2 basket	**Blueberries**

1) Slice the bananas and strawberries.
2) Toss all of the fruit in a bowl for a red white and blue salute.

Top with applesauce or a honey-lemon juice sauce if desired.

Serves 2-4

Peter Rabbit's Salad

Kids will hop for this one!

1 lg	Carrot
1½	Yellow apples
1/2 c	Raisins
1/3 c	Vanilla "soygurt"*
1 Tbl	Lemon juice
dash	Cinnamon
1/3 c	Chopped toasted walnuts (optional)

1) Grate the carrot and apple in a food processor.
2) Pour boiling water over the raisins to make them plump—
   strain after 5 minutes.
3) Toss all the ingredients together.

*Note: You can make your own vanilla soy yogurt by adding a bit
of vanilla extract and honey or maple syrup to plain soy yogurt.*

Mandala Salads

The visual arrangement of salads can be designed to symbolize the wheels of the universe. Constructing symmetrical artful salads can be a fun way to be creative and exceptionally delightful to delve into.

Traditionally, mandalas have been created by native folk peoples as an aid to meditation and as a vehicle for teaching their spiritual oneness with all. Creating mandalas is a ceremony in itself. See it as a sacred presentation for yourself and loved ones, each molecule of food being a crystal of love.

For a vegetable mandala, begin with a large platter or dish, and place spinach, lettuce or beet greens around the perimeter. Continue whirling this spiral flower with the vegetables that please you, such as finely shredded roots, julienne zucchinis, cucumber spears and sprouts. End in the center with something beautiful, like a radish "flower" (*see Rose bud diagram on page 61). For a fruit mandala, place lettuce leaves around perimeter, spiral fresh fruits in a pleasing pattern, and decorate with soaked dried fruit and nuts.

As you create a beautiful salad, remember that we too create our lives, what a gift!

Red Cabbage Slaw

This makes a large bowl of nourishing slaw, the Balsamic vinaigrette complements the red cabbage. An excellent source of fiber!

1 Lg	Carrot
1/2	Red cabbage
1/8	Green cabbage
1	Cucumber
	Few fresh sprigs of basil leaves

Balsamic Vinaigrette

2 Tbl	Lemon juice
1/4 c	Tofu Mayo (page 150)
1	Garlic clove, pressed
	Balsamic vinegar to thin

1) Shred the carrot and cabbages. Skin, seed and chop the cucumber, tear the basil leaves into small pieces.
2) Whisk or stir the sauce with a fork, and then toss all together.

Grated Beet Salad

Figure 1 beet per person. This salad is simple and refreshing!

4	Beets, grated (about 2 c)
3 Tbl	Dilled rice vinegar*
1½ Tbl	Fresh dill, chopped
	Add fresh green peas for a varied salad

Grate beets finely (a fine-shred food processor blade works the best), toss with vinegar then refrigerate.

*If you can't find the vinegar make your own by adding fresh or dried dill weed to natural rice vinegar, be sure to read the label since "seasoned" rice vinegar contains sugar.

Serves 4

Fennel Cabbage Slaw

*The fragrance of fresh herbs with the sweetness of fennel provides
a wonderful combination.*

2 sm	Zucchinis
1	Yellow crook neck squash
2	Carrots
1	Fennel bulb
1/2	Head cabbage
1 Tbl	Fresh dill, minced
1 Tbl	Toasted sun seeds (optional)

1) Slice the zucchini in rounds, julienne the squash, thinly slice the carrots, shred the fennel and cabbage.
2) Toss all of the ingredients in a bowl with **Creamy Dill Dressing** (page 109), add dill and sunflower seeds for a garnish.

Serves 6

Indian Carrot Salad

*This low calorie salad uses garam masala and soy yogurt
for a unique taste.*

3 lg	Carrots
1/3 c	Raisins, soaked in
2 Tbl	Apple juice
1	Banana, not too soft
1/2	Lemon, juiced
2 Tbl	Soy yogurt
1 tsp	Garam masala*, (page 156)

1) Shred the carrots finely in a food processor.
2) Soak the raisins in warmed apple juice for a few minutes to soften. Slice bananas.
3) Stir everything together. *Chill*

Serves 3

*Garam Masala *is an Indian seasoning blend of many flavors; it imparts a roasted, nutty, spicy taste.*

Ginger Lentil Sprout Salad

Crunchy, refreshing and vitamin packed, this Japanese flavored salad nestles mineral rich nori and hiziki seaweed with lentil sprouts for a great light meal.

2½ c	Sprouted lentils
1/2 c	Celery, finely chopped
1/2	Red onion, minced (about 1/3 c)
1 Tbl	Ginger, fresh, minced
1½ Tbl	Soy sauce (or tamari)
1/2 Tbl	Toasted Sesame oil—optional
1½ Tbl	Lemon juice
3 sheets	Nori, lightly toasted and torn into small pieces
1/4 c	Soaked hiziki

Toss and chill, garnish with minced green onions.

Serves 2-3

Chinese Snap Pea Salad

Simply delicious!

1/2 lb	**Snap peas, whole**
1 c	**Red peppers, sliced**
2 Tbl	**Brown sesame seeds**

Sauce

	Juice of 1 orange
1 Tbl	**Mellow white miso**
1	**Garlic clove, crushed**
1 tsp	**Honey or pure maple syrup or rice syrup**
1 tsp	**Rice vinegar**

1) Steam the peas for 5 minutes—they should be crisp tender.
2) Put the peas with the rest of the ingredients into a medium bowl.
3) Stir the sauce ingredients together then pour the sauce over the vegetables, refrigerate.

Serves 4

Sunflower Sprout Salad

2 c	**Sprouted sunflower seeds**
3/4 c	**Red cabbage, shredded**
3/4 c	**Green cabbage, diced**
1/4 c	**Cilantro leaves**
1/4 c	**Balsamic vinegar or Garlic Herb (fat-free) vinaigrette (page 99)**
	Cherry tomato halves as garnish

Toss all of the ingredients together, chill.

Serves 4-6

Mediterranean Eggplant Salad

This hearty salad goes well with crusty bread,
and a tossed green leaf salad.

1 lg	Whole eggplant, skinned and diced (about 1½ lb.)
1 med	Onion, diced
2	Garlic cloves, minced
1/4 c	Lemon juice
1 each	Red pepper and green pepper, julienne
1/4 c	Parsley, chopped
15 oz	Cooked garbanzo beans
2 Tbl	Olive oil
1 Tbl	Oregano
	Pinch of cayenne and sea salt

1) Steam the first two ingredients together until tender.
2) Toss the rest of the ingredients in a medium bowl, add the eggplant and onion, stir and refrigerate.

Serves 4-6

Marinated Vegetables

A great fat free snack.

1/2 head	Cauliflower, cut into florettes
1 c	Carrots, sliced thinly
1	Red onion, sliced thinly
1 c	Cherry tomatoes, halved
1 stalk	Broccoli, cut into florettes, peel and chop stems
4	Zucchinis, sliced (about 1 lb.)
1½ c	Garlic Herb (fat-free) Dressing (page 99)

1) Parboil the carrots and broccoli for no more than 2 minutes.
2) Toss the vegetables with 1½ cups of the dressing and chill several hours or overnight.

Makes a large bowl.

Cauliflower Almond Salad

A yummy salad with toasted almonds.

1 Big	Cauliflower
1/2 lg	Onion
1	Bell pepper, sliced
1/2 c	Almonds
2	Garlic cloves, pressed
1/2	Lemon, juiced
1 Tbl	Liquid aminos (or 1/2 Tbl tamari mixed with 1/2 Tbl filtered water)
1/4 c	Tofu Mayo (page 150)

1) Tear the cauliflower into florettes, slice the onion and steam them together for 3-5 minutes, rinse in cold filtered water.
2) Put the cauliflower and onion into a bowl with the bell peppers.
3) Chop and toast the almonds.
4) Toss all of the ingredients together and enjoy!

Serves 4

Coyote's Beet-loaf Salad

A nutritious blend of grated vegetables, nuts, tofu and spices formed into a festive southwestern shape. A complete meal in itself.

2	Beets
2	Carrots
1/4	Head cabbage
1	Zucchini (about 6" length)
4	Green onions
1	Bell pepper
1	Garlic clove, pressed
2 Tbl	Cilantro leaves
1/8 c	Liquid aminos
1/2 c	Sunflower seeds
1/4 c	Almonds
1/2 c	"Lite" Tofu
2 Tbl	Flax seeds
1/4 c	Nutritional yeast
1 tsp	Cumin
1/2 tsp each	Chile powder and sea salt

1) Shred all of the vegetables in a food processor or by hand.
2) Toast seeds lightly in an oven, then finely grind them in a blender—stop and stir occasionally until the seeds are ground.
3) Mix all of the ingredients in a bowl, then form into a cactus or moon shape; garnish with sliced olives, avocados, tomatoes and cilantro.

*Serve with **No-Oil Chips & Salsa** (page 122) and **Salsa Creme** dressing (page 105).*

Delphi Spinach Salad

A Greek spinach salad without the feta cheese.

1 bunch	Spinach
1/2	Cucumber, skinned
	Several cherry tomatoes, halved
6	Black olives, sliced
2 oz.	Soy cheese, crumbled (or "Savory Tofu" cubes)
3 Tbl	Sunflower seeds, freshly toasted
	Lemon wedges

1) Rinse, drain and pat the spinach leaves dry. Tear them into a large bowl or platter.
2) Add the sliced cucumbers, tomatoes and the rest of the ingredients.

*Serve with **Garlic Herb (fat-free) dressing** (page 99).*

Serves 2-3

Black-Eyed Pea Salad

The South meets the Southwest in this hearty salad.

4 c	Filtered water
1 c	Black-eyed Peas
4	Cloves of garlic, pressed
1	Bell pepper
1	Jalapeño, minced
1 sm	Onion, thinly sliced
1	Red pepper
1/2 tsp	Sea salt
1 tsp	Liquid aminos

1) Bring the filtered water to a boil, add the black-eyed peas.
2) Cover, return to a boil, then reduce heat and let sit 2 hours. Return pot to a boil, and simmer for 40 minutes.
3) Add the chopped peppers and the rest of the ingredients to the black-eyed peas, then toss all of the ingredients together and refrigerate.

Serves 4-6

Sprouted Soy Salad

A very nourishing salad.

- 3 c   **Soybean sprouts**
- 3   **Carrots (3 cups grated)**
- 1   **Bell pepper, chopped**

Dressing—1/2 Tbl freshly minced ginger, 2 Tbl Tamari, 3 Tbl Rice Vinegar, 2 tsp Toasted sesame oil, 1 Tbl Sesame seeds

1) Steam the soy sprouts for 3 minutes (available at oriental markets—or grow your own).
2) Finely grate the carrots. Stir the dressing ingredients together.
3) Toss all of the ingredients together in a medium sized bowl.

Serves 4

Three-Herb Tabouli

Quick and easy, a House favorite.

- 1 c   **Cracked wheat (Bulgar)**
- 3/4 c   **Boiling filtered water**
- 1 Tbl   **Olive oil**
- 3 Tbl   **Lemon juice**
- 4 lg   **Roma tomatoes, chopped**
- 1 c   **Parsley, freshly chopped**
- 2   **Scallions, minced**
- 1/2 c   **Fresh mint, minced**
- 1   **Garlic clove, pressed**
- 1 tsp   **Oregano**
-    **Cracked black pepper and sea salt to taste**

1) Put the cracked wheat into a medium bowl, stir in the boiling water and cover for 20 minutes.
2) Add the rest of the ingredients, toss well and chill.

Serve on a bed of baby greens or spinach leaves with sliced lemon wedges and cucumber spears.

Serves 4

Sprouted Lentil Loaf

Salad:

1	Celery stock (use inner soft ribs and leaves only)
1/2	Red onion (1/3-1/2 cup chopped)
1½ c	Lentil sprouts
2	Carrots (medium size, about 1 cup grated)
1/2	Zucchini (about 1/3 cup grated)

Sauce:

1/3 c	Tofu Mayo (page 150)
3 Tbl	Lemon juice
2 tsp	Soy sauce or liquid aminos
1	Garlic clove
2 tsp	Dill weed and coriander (if fresh use 1 Tbl each)
	Dash of cumin, curry and cayenne

1) Pulse chop the celery and onion finely in a food processor. Add the lentil sprouts and pulse chop one to three quick times (do not mash).
2) Change the blade to a fine grate, grate the carrots and zucchinis into the same work bowl. Transfer vegetables to a salad bowl.
3) Blend the sauce ingredients together, toss the sauce into the salad—form into a loaf and garnish (or keep as a tossed salad), chill.

Serves 4

Herbed Wheatberry Salad

1½ c	**Soft wheat berries***
5½ c	**Filtered water**
2	**Cloves of garlic**
1 lg	**Red onion**
1 Tbl	**Olive oil**
2	**Medium carrots**
1	**Celery rib**
1	**Lemon, juiced**
1/4 c	**Peas**
1/2 tsp	**Sea salt**
1 tsp	**Dill weed**
	Fresh dill sprigs for garnish

1) Rinse the wheat berries. Bring the water to a boil in a medium pot.
2) Add the wheat berries, return to a boil and simmer for 1 hour, or until soft.
3) Press the garlic, chop the onion, and sauté them in oil and lemon juice until soft (2 minutes). Add them to the cooked wheat berries.
4) Grate the carrots, slice the celery.
5) Toss all of the ingredients into a bowl and chill.

Serve with a garnish of marinated tomatoes and mushrooms.

Serves 4-6

*2 types of wheat berries are available: soft and hard. Use the soft ones for cooking. The hard ones are for sprouting wheat grass or grinding into flour.

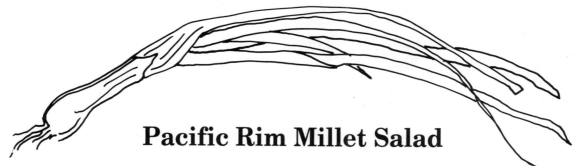

Pacific Rim Millet Salad

A spicy fragrant tofu and millet salad, delicious as a main course or lunch. Millet is high in protein and is a non-mucus forming grain.

2 c	Cooked millet*
1 c	Cubed firm tofu, marinated**
1	Red pepper, julienne
1	Lime, juiced
1	Lemon, juiced
1	Jalapeño, roasted, seeded and minced (optional)
1	Garlic clove, pressed
1 tsp	Fresh ginger, minced
2	Green onions, slivered on angle
2 Tbl	Sesame oil
1 Tbl	Toasted sesame seeds
2 tsp	Liquid aminos (or to taste)

Toss together all of the ingredients and chill.

Serves 2-3

*To prepare millet, rinse 1 cup of millet in filtered water, then stir into a pot of 2 cups boiling water. Cover the pot, turn to low heat and let it steam for 15 minutes or until tender. Fluff with a fork.

**or use "savory tofu," found in the refrigerated section in natural food stores. Or, you may marinate firm tofu in 1 Tbl of tamari.

Spanish Rice Salad

Fragrant rice sautéed in salsa with zucchinis.

3/4 c	**Long grain rice (jasmine or basmati)**
1/2	**Lemon, juiced**
1½ c	**Filtered water or broth**
1 tsp	**Cumin seeds**
1/4 c	**Salsa Fresca (page 144)**
	(fresh chunkie kind)
1	**Garlic, pressed**
2-3	**Zucchinis, sliced**
1 tsp	**Coriander**
	Tamari to taste

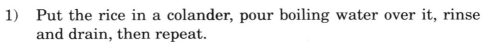

1) Put the rice in a colander, pour boiling water over it, rinse and drain, then repeat.
2) Squeeze the lemon on top of the rice and cover for 10 minutes or until rice softens.
3) Heat a skillet, add the rice, continue stirring until the rice begins to get slightly brown.
4) Add the cumin, salsa and garlic; continue stirring then add the filtered water or broth, zucchinis and tamari, cover for 15 minutes.
5) Fluff the rice with a fork when the rice is done.
6) Put the rice into a bowl and toss with:

2-3	**Sprigs fresh chopped Basil leaves**
1 Tbl	**toasted sesame seeds**
1	**Tomato, seeded and chopped**
	Sliced green olives to taste

7) Spoon rice salad onto plates lined with lettuce leaves.

Three-Pepper Black Bean

A festive and fragrant salad, dotted with yellow, red and green peppers.

2 c	Cooked black beans
1	Garlic clove, pressed
1/2" piece of	Ginger, grated
2/3 c	Yellow pepper, chopped
2/3 c	Green pepper, chopped
2/3 c	Red pepper, chopped
1/4 c	Cilantro leaves, chopped
3	Green onions, minced
1 Tbl each	Vinegar and liquid aminos
1	Lime, juiced
	Crack pepper to taste (if you like spicy—add cayenne or minced jalapeño)
1	Cucumber
2	Tomatoes

1) Put the beans into a medium bowl, add the garlic, ginger, peppers, and cilantro.
2) Add the rest of the spices, stir well and chill.

Before serving:
3) Seed, skin and chop the cucumber in half moons, wedge the tomatoes.
4) On a serving platter lay a ring of sprouts, put the bean salad in the center then arrange the tomatoes and cucumbers around the perimeter.

Serves 4-6

Marinated Bean Salad

To turn this dish into a sensational main dish salad; spoon marinated beans over a bed of shredded greens, chopped tomatoes and peppers. Serve with your choice of dressing.

1½ c	Baby lima beans (you can use any beans)
1 Tbl	Minced ginger
2	Garlic cloves, chopped
	Bay leaf

1) Cover the beans with filtered water and soak them overnight.
2) Rinse the beans, cover them with fresh filtered water and bring to a boil. Add the ginger, garlic and bay, then reduce to simmer for 45 minutes to 1 hour until al dente (not mushy soft).
3) Drain the beans in a colander and rinse in cold filtered water.
4) Put the beans in a large bowl and toss with:

2	Garlic cloves, pressed
2 Tbl	Olive oil
1 Tbl	Italian herbs (a mix of oregano, basil, rosemary and thyme)
1/2	Lemon juiced, with thinly sliced sections for garnish
1/4 tsp	Sea salt
1 Tbl	Liquid aminos
2 Tbl	Red wine vinegar

Santa Fe Tempeh Salad

For a festive summer meal try this salad with
No-Oil Chips & Salsa *(page 122),* **Party Black Bean Dip** *(page 146),*
fresh fruit or **Yucatan Salad** *(page 63).*

8 oz	Tempeh, steamed 5 minutes
1 lg	Garlic clove, pressed
2 Tbl	Tamari or liquid aminos
1/4 tsp	Cayenne (or 1/2 jalapeño, minced)
1/2 tsp	Chile powder
1/2 c	Almonds, roasted then chopped
1 lg	Tomato, chopped
1	Bell pepper, thinly slice
1/2 bunch	Cilantro, chopped (about 1/4 c)
2	Limes, juiced
1/2	Red onion, minced
2	Tangerines, sectioned and peeled

1) Cube the steamed tempeh, pour the next 4 ingredients over the tempeh and toss together—let it marinate an hour or two or overnight.
2) Chop all of the veggies and toss the tempeh together with the remaining ingredients in a large container—chill.

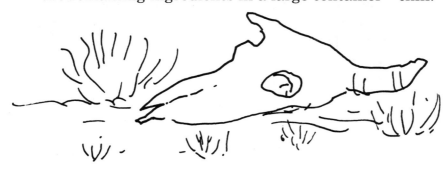

Salad for a Mermaid

1 c	Hiziki seaweed
1½ c	Peas
3 small	Carrots
1/2 c	Tofu, cut in 1/2" cubes
	A few cilantro leaves, chopped

Sauce

2 Tbl	Tamari
1/4 c	Fresh ginger
1½ tsp	Toasted sesame oil
1 tsp	Wasabi powder
1	Green onion
1/2 c	Filtered water
1/4 c	Lemon juice
1 Tbl	Sesame tahini
2 tsp	Honey

1) Soak hiziki in hot filtered water for 10 minutes, rinse and drain 2 times.
2) Steam the peas for a few minutes until tender.
3) Cut the carrots into "sticks and flowers." *See diagram in* **Culinary Decorations** (page 61).
4) Blend the sauce ingredients in a blender until smooth. Strain the sauce over the salad (discard the fiber in the strainer), toss salad.

Chill.

Serves 2

Citrus Pasta Salad

A refreshing yet fiery salad full of unusual tastes.

4 oz	Fresh spaghetti or soba noodles
2	Oranges, peeled and chopped
1/2 c	Nopalitos*, diced
1 c	Pineapple chunks, fresh
1	Lime, juiced
1/2-1	Jalapeño, minced

1) Cook pasta al dente, rinse and drain.
2) Toss the pasta with the remaining ingredients, and be prepared for a very exotic experience.

Noplatios are cactus pads, usually found skinned and diced in the Mexican section of markets.

Veggie Rotelli in Parsley Sauce

10 oz	Rotelli pasta
1 c	Mushrooms, sliced*
2 fat	Tomatoes, seeded and chopped
1/2 c	Black olives, sliced
1	Green pepper, thinly sliced into ribs

Sauce:

1 c	Parsley without stems
3	Green onions, sliced
1/3 c	Lemon juice
1/2 Tbl	Dijon mustard
1 tsp each	Honey and onion powder
2 Tbl	Tofu Mayo (page 150)
	Cracked pepper

1) Cook rotellis al dente—rinse and drain.
2) Put the vegetables into a large bowl, add the pasta.
3) Blend the sauce ingredients in a blender until smooth, pour over the pasta. Stir together

Mushrooms can be simmered in 1 tsp olive oil and garlic before adding to pasta.

Serves 4-6

Tortellinis with Seasonal Vegetables

16 oz	Tortellini pasta (vegetable)
2	Garlic cloves, pressed
1 Tbl	Red wine and 1 Tbl filtered water
1	Lemon, juiced
2 c	Sliced mushrooms
1/2 sm	Eggplant, cubed
1/2 lg	Onion
1/4 c	Liquid aminos
2 Tbl	Pinenuts, toasted
	Cracked pepper
2 Tbl each	Olive oil (optional), red wine vinegar

1) Cook the tortellinis until tender, rinse and drain.
2) Sauté the garlic in wine, lemon and filtered water. Add the mushrooms, eggplant, chopped onion and liquid aminos. When the vegetables are almost tender, put them into a large bowl.
3) Toss together with the remaining ingredients—adjust the seasonings, refrigerate.

Pesto Pasta Salad

This is delicious. It makes a pretty summer meal.

1 lb	Pasta (tortellinis, rotellis or elbows)
1/4 c	Pesto, (page 149)
1	Red bell pepper, sliced
1	Yellow bell pepper, sliced
1/2 c	Walnuts or pecans, toasted and chopped
1/4 c	Rice vinegar or lime juice

1) Cook the pasta al dente, mix the vinegar with the pesto.
2) Stir all of the ingredients together, chill.

Serves 4

Hiziki & Ramen Sea Noodle Salad

Seaweed and oriental noodles are nestled among salad and spices.

8 oz	**Ramen or soba**
	Several Kale leaves
1 small head	**Cabbage, shredded**
1/2 c	**Hiziki (soak in 3/4 cup filtered water for 15 minutes, drain)**
3	**Green onions, minced**
1 tsp	**Ginger, skinned and minced**
1	**Carrot, grated**
dash	**Cayenne**

Sauce:

3 Tbl	**Tamari**
2 tsp	**Toasted sesame oil**
3 Tbl	**Rice vinegar**
2 Tbl	**Brown sesame seeds**

1) Cook the soba, when al dente add the kale and cabbage to the filtered water. Cover for a couple of minutes, then drain and rinse (or save stock for a soup).

2) Prepare hiziki, blend sauce, and toss all of the ingredients together.

*Serve with **Ginger Sesame Marinade** (page 100) on the side if desired. Garnish with curly endive and a flower.*

Serves 4

Thai-bright Salad

A classic Thai salad of bean thread noodles, mint, lime and shredded vegetables.

2 oz	Bean thread noodles
2	Carrots
1/2	Jicama
1 Tbl	Lime juice and grated skin
2 Tbl	Rice vinegar
1 Tbl	Rice syrup
1/4 c	Torn mint leaves (loose pack)
1/4 c	Cilantro leaves (loose pack)
dash	Red chile flakes, sesame oil and tamari
2 Tbl	Minced peanuts

1) Soak the noodles in boiling water for 10 minutes until al dente.
2) Shred the carrots and dice the jicama. Put the veggies into a bowl along with the noodles.
3) Mix the next 3 ingredients, pour over the veggies.
4) Toss all of the ingredients together and smile!

Serves 2

Simple Soba Salad

5 dried	Shiitake mushrooms
6 oz	Soba (buckwheat) noodles
3½ Tbl	Tamari
2 Tbl	Sesame oil, cold pressed
2 Tbl	Rice vinegar
1 Tbl	Honey
1 Tbl	Hot pepper oil—(toasted sesame oil)
6	Scallions, minced
2 Tbl	Black sesame seeds

1) Cover the shiitake mushrooms with filtered water, and let them soak for 10 minutes. Slice them when they are soft (remove stems).
2) Cook soba according to directions on pack, or until al dente. Toss the soba in a large bowl with the rest of the ingredients.
3) Decorate with carrot stars if desired—cut "V" shapes out of a carrot lengthwise, then slice into "stars" (page 62).

Marinated Tofu in Soba Noodles

This is a cross between a soup and a salad and makes a wonderful light meal.

4 oz	Firm tofu cut in 1/2" thick slices (figure a 2 oz slice per serving)
4 oz	Soba noodles, cooked and drained
2 Tbl	Chopped cilantro leaves
6	Cherry tomatoes, halved
1 c	Sprouts (radish, alfalfa and clover), chopped
2 tsp	Toasted sesame seeds

Marinade:

1/4 c	Mirin cooking sake
1/4 c	Soy sauce
1 tsp	Ginger, skinned and freshly minced
	Cayenne

1) Stir the marinade together and spoon it over the tofu, let it sit for as long as you can, it's still great if you don't have any time to wait.
2) Put the tofu into a toaster oven and broil it for 10 minutes or so.
3) Put the soba noodles into individual deep bowls.
4) Lay the tofu and its sizzling juices on top, then garnish with salad goodies.

Serve with a Japanese spoon and chopsticks.

Serves 2

Pasta Oriental

1 lb	Fusilli pasta
1/2 head	Cabbage, coarsely shredded)
1/2 lg	Onion
10	Shiitake mushrooms (soak in filtered water for 15 minutes if dried, remove stems)
1 15 oz can	Palm hearts, sliced
1 small can	Water chestnuts, quartered
1 can	Baby corns
1	Red pepper thinly sliced

Sauté sauce for mushrooms and onions:

2 Tbl each	Filtered water and Tamari
1 Tbl each	Honey, Mirin and minced, skinned ginger root
dash	Cayenne and toasted sesame oil

1) Cook the pasta until al dente, turn off the heat, then add the cabbage to the pot. After a few minutes, drain and rinse.
2) Slice the onions and mushrooms, simmer in the sauté sauce for 10 minutes covered on low heat.
3) Toss all of the ingredients together in a big bowl with:

3	Garlic cloves, pressed
1/2	Lemon, juiced
	Tamari to taste

Garnish top with cilantro leaves and sesame seeds.

Serves 6-8

Tropical Tempeh Salad in Cantaloupe Shells

1/2 pack	Tempeh, chopped (4 oz)
2 Tbl	Liquid aminos
2 small	Cantaloupes, halved and seeded
1/2	Lemon, juiced
2 Tbl	Coconut shreds
1 tsp	Curry powder
1 lg	Spoonful soy yogurt

1) Marinate the tempeh for 1 hour in the liquid aminos, then steam for 15 minutes.
2) Scoop out the melon into balls or chunks. Slice the bottom off of each half of the melon so it can sit correctly.
3) Put the melon balls in a bowl with the rest of the ingredients, toss.
4) Adjust the seasonings to taste and fill up the melon bowls, garnish with chives, lemon twists, raisins, or toasted nuts.

Serves 2-4

SALADS DRESSINGS

Purifying = Dressings on the light side with vegetables and juices
Fortifying = Heartier dressings using nuts, tofu, tofumayo, vinegars
                   or oils.
Sweet = Sauces for fruit or desserts.

♥ Fat Free

SALAD DRESSINGS

The right salad dressing can push your taste buds right into a sublime realm of ecstasy, boost nutrition and complete the protein of your favorite salad.

We've provided a broad range of healthy tastes in these dressings; those prepared with tofu, with sprouted or toasted nuts and seeds, without any oils or fats using all vegetables and juices, and a few light vinaigrettes using some pure virgin oils.

Salad dressings are fun and easy to make, and so much tastier and better for you than the store bought ones.

Treat yourself special while preparing food, keep a gardenia in
a vase to fill up the air with heaven.

Golden Temple Dressing

These are purifying and delicious!

1 c	Fresh carrot juice
1	Garlic clove, chopped
1/4 med	Avocado*
1/2	Lemon, juiced
1 tsp	Ginger, skinned and minced

Blend until smooth.

Rose Temple Dressing

1 c	Beet juice
1	Garlic clove, chopped
1/4 med	Avocado*
1/2	Lemon, juiced
1 tsp	Ginger, skinned and minced

Blend until smooth.

Avocados are very high in fat, so use them sparingly.

Sprouted Almond Sauce

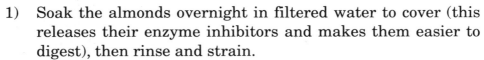

1 c	Almonds
1½ c	Filtered water
1	Lemon, juiced
1	Garlic clove, pressed
1 Tbl	Rice vinegar
1 Tbl	Nutritional yeast
2 Tbl	Liquid aminos
dash	Cayenne and curry

1) Soak the almonds overnight in filtered water to cover (this releases their enzyme inhibitors and makes them easier to digest), then rinse and strain.

2) Blend the almonds and filtered water in a blender until smooth; add the rest of the ingredients and blend again. (Add filtered water if necessary).

Yields about 1½ cups

Sprouted Sun Seed Sauce

A delicious and purifying dressing.

1¼ c	Sprouted sunflower seeds
4	Garlic cloves, chopped
1/4 c	Lemon juice
2 Tbl	Liquid aminos
1 c	Filtered water
dash	Cayenne

1) Put all of the ingredients in the blender, add the filtered water last, thin to desired consistency.

2) Blend until smooth, chill.

Divine over steamed vegetables, or in a pita sandwich.

Garlic Herb (fat free)

A wonderful no-oil fat free vinaigrette.
Use as a marinade for vegetables.

2 c	Filtered water
1/4 tsp	Agar flakes
5 Tbl	Balsamic or cider vinegar
1½ Tbl	Garlic, chopped
2	Green onions, chopped
2 tsp	Onion powder
1 tsp each	Coriander, basil, oregano
1/2 tsp	Cracked black pepper
1 tsp	Barley malt syrup or honey

1) Dissolve the agar in the filtered water then transfer to a pot. Bring the agar-water mixture to a boil for 1 minute then pour it into a blender.
2) Add the rest of the ingredients, blend and refrigerate. Whisk before serving.

Yields about 2½ cups

Orange Miso Dressing

Great on cabbage slaws and chilled bean salads.

1 c	Orange juice
3 Tbl	Mellow white miso
3 sm	Garlic cloves, chopped
1 Tbl	Honey or maple syrup
1 Tbl	Rice vinegar

Blend until smooth, chill.

Yields about 1⅓ cups

Ginger Sesame Marinade

A fat free Asian Vinaigrette.

2 c	Filtered water
1 tsp	Agar flakes
6 Tbl	Rice vinegar
2 Tbl	Ginger, skinned and chopped
1/4 c	Honey
2 Tbl	Tamari
2 Tbl	Brown sesame seeds
	A few drops of toasted sesame oil

1) In a small saucepan soak the agar in the filtered water until it dissolves. Bring it to a boil, then remove the pan from the heat and pour the agar into a blender.
2) Add the vinegar and ginger, blend them well and strain away the fibers.
3) Add the rest of the ingredients to the blender, continue blending, then refrigerate.

Yields about 2¾ cups

Avocado Sauce

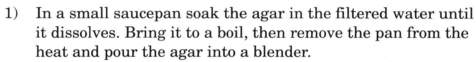

Great on coleslaw and salads, but rich.

1	Avocado, mashed
1/4 c	Cilantro leaves, packed
2	Garlic cloves, chopped
1/4 c	Lemon juice
1 Tbl	Liquid aminos
1/2 tsp	Cumin
dash	Cayenne
1¼ c	Filtered water

Blend in a blender until soft and silky.

Yields about 1¾ cups

Alive Salad Sauce

This is purifying and zippy.

2	Lemons, juiced
1	Garlic clove, chopped
1 Tbl	Ginger, skinned and freshly chopped
2 Tbl	Liquid aminos
1½ Tbl	Nutritional yeast
1 Tbl	Tahini
1 tsp	Honey or barley malt syrup

Blend.

Yields about 3/4 cup

Tomato Tahini

1½ c	Tomato juice
1/2	Lemon, juiced
2	Garlic cloves, chopped
1	Jalapeño (seed first of you don't like "hot")
1½ Tbl	Tahini
1 Tbl	Nutritional yeast
1/2 Tbl	Liquid aminos
	Cracked pepper
2 Tbl	Onion, chopped

Blend all of the ingredients until smooth and creamy, adjust seasonings to taste.

Yields about 2 cups

24 Carrot Sauce

Delicious! One of our favorites.

1 c	Carrot juice
1/2	Lemon juiced
1/4 c	"Lite" tofu
2 Tbl	Tofu mayo (page 150)
2	Garlic cloves, pressed
1/2 tsp	Dill weed
2 Tbl	Balsamic vinegar
	Tamari and cayenne to taste

Blend in a blender until smooth.

Yields about 1⅔ cups

Honey Mustard Vinaigrette

A tart and spicy low-cal vinaigrette, great over coleslaws.

1/2 c	Red wine vinegar
2 Tbl	Tarragon mustard*
2 Tbl	Lemon juice
2 Tbl	Honey

Whisk together in a small bowl.

Yields 1 cup

*or use regular mustard with a pinch of tarragon added.

Spicy Thousand Island

Adds zest and a beautiful color to salads.

1/2 c	Natural ketchup mixed with 1/2 cup filtered water
1/2 c	Tofu Mayo (page 150)
2 Tbl	Salsa Fresca (page 144)
1½	Lemons, juiced
2	Garlic cloves, chopped

Blend in a blender until creamy. Add filtered water to desired consistency.

Yields about 1¾ cups

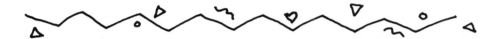

Almond Ginger Sauce

Great as a dip or salad dressing, on potatoes or steamed veggies.
Highly nutritious.

1 c	Almonds, soaked (soak 1/2 cup of almonds in filtered water overnight)
2 Tbl	Almonds, roasted
1¾ c	Broth or filtered water
2	Garlic cloves, chopped
1 Tbl	Ginger, skinned and freshly chopped
1 Tbl	Soy sauce or tamari
2 Tbl	Lemon juice
1/8 tsp	Cayenne (or to taste)

1) Put 1/2 cup of raw almonds into a jar and cover them with filtered water. Let the almonds soak for 10 hours.
2) Rinse and drain the almonds. Put all of the ingredients into a blender and puree for a couple of minutes, until creamy.

Yields 2½ cups

Jalapeño Dill Creme

Sesame tahini and soft tofu are blended to form a creamy base for this exciting sauce.

1 c	"Lite" tofu
1 Tbl	Tahini
1	Jalapeño (seeded of you don't like hot)
1 tsp	Dill weed
1	Garlic clove
1 Tbl	Lemon juice
dash	Tamari to taste
	(Add a couple of drops of toasted sesame oil if a more prominent sesame taste is desired)

1) Blend all of the ingredients in a blender until the mixture is soft and silky.
2) Garnish with toasted sesame seeds, dill or lemon slivers.

Use as a sauce for rice or vegetables, salad dressing or dip.

Yields 3/4 cup

Salsa Creme

A spicy creamy salad dressing.

1/4 c	Salsa Fresca (page 144)
1/2 c	Silken "Lite" tofu, crumbled
1	Juicy lemon or lime
1 Tbl	Soy yogurt or Tofu mayo (page 150)
1/2 Tbl	Liquid aminos
1/2 tsp	Honey

Blend until creamy.

Yields 3/4 cup

Yogurt Tahini

Delicious as a dressing, a sauce for falafel sandwiches, or over pasta.

8 oz	Soy yogurt, plain
3 Tbl	Tahini
1	Lemon, juiced
2	Garlic cloves, chopped
1 Tbl	Mellow white miso
1/4 c	Fresh parsley leaves, minced
	Cracked black pepper

Blend all of the ingredients together until smooth.

Yields 3/4 cup

Tofu Sesame Sauce

1 c	Silken "Lite" tofu
1 Tbl	Tahini
1/2	Lemon, juiced (about 2 Tbl)
2 Tbl	Toasted sesame seeds
2 Tbl	Chopped onion (or 2 tsp powder)
1	Garlic clove, pressed
1/2 tsp	Honey
2 tsp	Tamari
1/4 c	Filtered water

1) Blend the tofu, tahini and lemon juice in a blender.
2) Slowly add the filtered water and the rest of the ingredients.
3) Blend until smooth.

Yields 1½ cups

Chile Peanut Sauce

Try over a Mexican salad or coleslaw featuring bell peppers, jicama, cabbage and carrots; yields 1¼ cups.

1 c	Tomato juice
1 Tbl	Peanut butter
3/4 tsp	Chile powder
1 Tbl	Lemon juice
1	Garlic clove, chopped
dash	Cayenne

1) Blend until smooth.
2) Tomato juice can be replaced with 3 Tbl natural ketchup diluted with 3/4 cup filtered water.

Italian Herbal Vinaigrette

Nutritious spirulina turns this vinaigrette green.

1/4 c	Olive oil, cold pressed
1/4 c	Lemon juice
1/4 c	Apple cider vinegar
1/4 c	Filtered water
2 Tbl	Sun seeds or pinenuts, toasted
2 Tbl	Soy Parmesan cheese
1 tsp	Spirulina
1/2 tsp	Oregano and basil
2	Garlic cloves, chopped
1/4 tsp	Black pepper
dash	Sea salt

Blend until smooth. Freshly toasted sun seeds have the best flavor.

Yields 1¼ cups

Spinach Dressing

1/2 bunch	Spinach, steamed 3 minutes
1/8 c	Sun seeds, toasted
2	Garlic cloves, pressed
1/2	Lemon, juiced
1/3	Jalapeño, minced
1 tsp	Onion powder
	Filtered water to thin, tamari to taste

Put all of the ingredients into a blender, blend until smooth and creamy.

Yields about 1¼ cups

Toasted Lime Dressing

Delicious—especially nice on spinach salads with shredded red cabbage, radish sprouts and cucumbers.

1/2 c	Silken "Lite" tofu, crumbled
1/4 c	Sunflower seeds
1/2 c	Filtered water
3	Green onions
3	Limes
3 Tbl	Rice vinegar
1	Garlic clove, chopped
1 Tbl	Eggless mayo or Tofu mayo (page 150)
1 Tbl	Liquid aminos

1) Toast the sun seeds to a light brown.
2) Coarse chop the onions, juice the limes.
3) Blend all of the ingredients together in a blender, until smooth.

Yields about 1½ cups

Creamy Dill

A high protein, low calorie, delicious green dressing.

1 c	Silken "Lite" tofu
2 Tbl	Tofunaise or Tofu mayo (page 150)
1/4 c	Lemon juice, fresh
1 tsp	Onion powder
1/4 c	Fresh dill leaves
2 Tbl	Wine vinegar
1 Tbl	Apple juice
2 Tbl	Pinenuts or sunflower seed, toasted

Blend until smooth and then chill.

Yields 2 cups

Yogurtnaise

A zesty soy yogurt mayo.

1/2	Lemon, juiced (or 3 Tbl)
1/2 c	Soy yogurt, plain
2 Tbl	Herb red wine vinegar or apple cider vinegar
1	Garlic clove, pressed
dash	Cayenne and aminos

Blend until smooth.

Yields about 7/8 cup

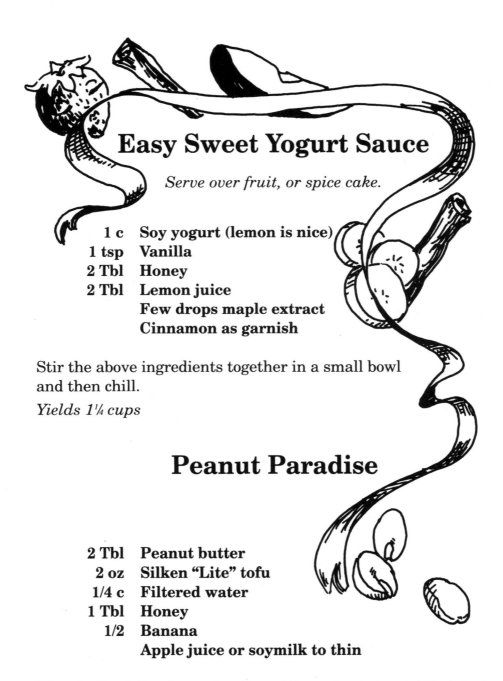

Easy Sweet Yogurt Sauce

Serve over fruit, or spice cake.

1 c	Soy yogurt (lemon is nice)
1 tsp	Vanilla
2 Tbl	Honey
2 Tbl	Lemon juice
	Few drops maple extract
	Cinnamon as garnish

Stir the above ingredients together in a small bowl and then chill.

Yields 1¼ cups

Peanut Paradise

2 Tbl	Peanut butter
2 oz	Silken "Lite" tofu
1/4 c	Filtered water
1 Tbl	Honey
1/2	Banana
	Apple juice or soymilk to thin

Blend all of the ingredients, adding the juice to the desired thickness. Can be used as a delicious drink or shake by adding more apple juice and some crushed ice.

Yields about 1½ cups

Coco Lime Fruit Glaze

A very refreshing sauce for fruit salads.

1/4 c	Lime juice
2 Tbl	Honey
2 Tbl	Thick coconut milk (Lowfat: use soymilk with a drop of coconut extract added)

Whisk together.

Yields about 1/2 cup

Sauce of Angels

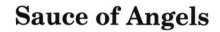

Delicious with cakes or over fruit gels.

1 c	Silken "Lite" tofu
1/4 c	Fructose
1 tsp	Vanilla
	soy milk to thin

Blend in a blender until smooth.

Yields about 1¼ cups

Fruity Tofu Creme Sauce

Serve on the side with your fruit salads.

1 pk	Silken "Lite" tofu
3 Tbl	Lemon juice
4 Tbl	Natural fruit syrup (raspberry or strawberry)
1/2 tsp	Vanilla
1/2 tsp	Lemon peel, grated
1/3 c	Orange juice
1 tsp	Poppy seeds

Purée until smooth.

Yields about 1¾ cups

FUN FOODS

♥ Fat Free

FUN FOODS

Healthy Snacks and appetite teasers are *fun* foods. The kind of thing you serve at a party when everyone stands around the kitchen eating and talking, or when you curl up in bed to read, or watch a movie. These light meals have much versatility, so you can spread, dip and sprinkle anything on them that sounds good to you.

Fun foods are the perfect companion for solitary nibbling, seductive noshes for intimate twosomes, or full on party foods for large gatherings.

Whatever the occasion, these foods are fun!

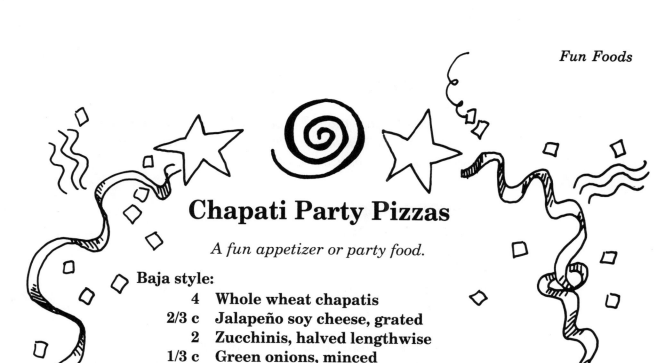

Chapati Party Pizzas

A fun appetizer or party food.

Baja style:

4	**Whole wheat chapatis**
2/3 c	**Jalapeño soy cheese, grated**
2	**Zucchinis, halved lengthwise**
1/3 c	**Green onions, minced**
1	**Roasted red bell pepper, cut into strips**
	Fresh cilantro, chopped
	Salsa Fresca (page 144)

1) Slice the zucchinis into 1/4" thick slabs, and steam them until crisp-tender.
2) Toast the chapatis in the oven on a cookie sheet until just crisp, not brown, then remove them from the oven.
3) Cover the chapatis with grated soy cheese, zucchini strips, more soy cheese, green onions and red peppers.
4) Toast or broil until the soy cheese melts—3-5 minutes.
5) Serve with salsa swirled on top, add cilantro leaves as a garnish.

For variation, try adding one of the following after the soy cheese is melted on top:

Italian—*Add sliced olives, marinara sauce, basil leaves, sliced tofu pups and garlic.*

Mexican—*Add avocado slices, black beans, **Red Chile Sauce**, (page 129).*

Thai—*Add crushed peanuts, cilantro, mint, red chili flakes, and **Tofu Thai Peanut Sauce**, (page 138).*

Have fun experimenting!

Serves 4

Potato Latkes

Dairyless, eggless potato pancakes. Serve with either apple sauce and soy yogurt, marinara sauce or ketchup, or garnish with sliced tomatoes and dill.

3/4 c	"Lite" soy milk, plain
1/2 c	Silken "Lite" tofu
3 Tbl	Whole wheat flour
1 Tbl	Onion powder
2 sm	Potatoes, scrubbed
1/4	Onion

1) Purée the tofu in a blender, add the soy milk.
2) Shred or grate the potatoes and onion in a food processor, squeeze and blot the mixture dry.
3) Put the tofu and vegetables into a bowl, stir in the tofu mixture.
4) Pour the mixture onto a hot oiled griddle and flip the latkes when brown.

Eggplant Rounds

A curry paste gets brushed on top of eggplant slices and broiled for a quick treat.

1 sm	Eggplant, sliced in rounds 1/2" thick
1 tsp	Curry powder
1/4 tsp each	Cumin, coriander, onion powder
1 tsp	Liquid aminos
	Lemon juice
	Filtered water as needed
1/2 tsp	Olive oil

1) Stir the spices together to make a paste—brush the paste on the eggplants.
2) Broil for several minutes until the eggplants are tender.

Lo-Cal Popcorn

Mix air popped popcorn with nutritional yeast, liquid aminos, cayenne, lemon juice and whatever spices delight you—dill and curry are great! Or, using a small spray bottle, spray the popcorn with a mixture of:

3 parts	Tamari or liquid aminos
1 part	Filtered water
dash	Lemon juice

Then sprinkle on nutritional yeast and spices. (The spices stick better to the popcorn this way.)

Baked Tofu Rice Balls

These make yummy snacks that can be eaten hot or cold.

2 c	Brown rice, cooked (or leftover)
1	Garlic clove, pressed
2/3 lb	Silken "Lite" tofu
1 Tbl	Onion powder
1/2 c	Almonds, toasted
3 Tbl	Oat bran
1/4 tsp	Sea salt

1) Put all of the ingredients into a food processor and mix together on pulse chop until everything is evenly distributed.
2) Roll the mixture into small 1½" round balls. Roll the balls into your desired coating:
   Onion powder and diced onions
   Seasoned bread crumbs
3) Bake 30 minutes at 400°.

*Serve with **Spicy Cilantro Dipping Sauce**—(page 145).*

Makes 24-30 balls

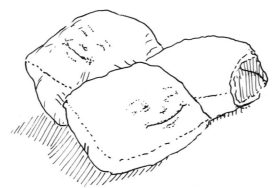

Mochi Puffs

Sold in many gourmet and natural foods stores, mochi is a sweet glutinous rice formed into a flat cake. Break it apart into 2" squares and toast it until it puffs up and gets browned. A chewy delicious snack.

1 pack **Mochi, (makes 9, 2" squares)**
Spicy Cilantro Dipping Sauce (page 145).

1) Preheat oven at 450°.
2) Break apart the mochi, place them on the top rack of an oven. Bake the mochi squares until they puff up and are toasty (about 10 minutes).
3) Arrange the mochi puffs on a serving platter, serve them with the sauce in the center.

Option: fill mochi puffs with the tofu stuffing from page 245.

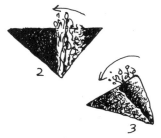

122

Nori Toastitos

Nori is a perfect diet food, for it is a low calorie non-fat mineral rich "tortilla" that will hold any foods of your imagination. Have fun creating a salad and sauce smörgasbord inside your nori roll.

Nori sushi sheets
Sprouts of choice (buckwheat, sunflower, alfalfa)
Steamed carrot sticks, whole peas or
other veggies
Your favorite sauce or dressing,
(or go traditional with wasabi paste and tamari)

Place veggies on half of the nori sheet and roll up jellyroll style, sealing end with water. Or, cut the nori sheet into a triangle and roll up like a cone.

Have fun rolling your own!

No-oil Chips & Salsa

Make your chips and salsa a healthy occasion by not frying them.

> **12   Corn tortillas**
> **1 recipe   Salsa Fresca (page 144) or Cactus Salsa (page 143)**

1) Toast whole tortillas on the rack of an oven for 10-15 minutes until crisp (who needs all that oil?).
2) Break apart in 1/4's and serve around a center bowl of salsa.

*Bring out the **Party Black Bean Dip** (page 146) for a real feast.*

Mexican Flag Seed Cheese Nachos

An enzyme-rich nacho treat.

Per person

1	**Corn tortilla**
2 Tbl	**Seed Cheese (page 151)**
2 Tbl	**Salsa (page 144)**
	Several black olives, sliced
	Cilantro, fresh, to garnish

1) Toast the tortillas in the oven for a couple of minutes until crunchy.
2) Spread the seed cheese on top, pour salsa on next, then garnish with the olives and cilantro, olé!

Serves 1

Crispy Baked Wontons

*A delightful party appetizer that's not fried. Serve with **Spicy Cilantro Dipping Sauce** (page 145) or **Tofu Thai Peanut Sauce** (page 138).*

Follow the recipe for **Wontons in Kombu Broth** (page 273), up to step 6 until cooked al dente, strain the wontons onto a platter. Meanwhile preheat your oven to broil. Lightly oil a ventilated rack (or use a non-stick baking sheet) and place the wontons on top. Broil the wontons until light brown, turn with tongs and broil the other side.

These will take about 10-15 minutes to bake each side. Keep an eye on them. Serve them hot, right out of the oven.

SAUCES, DIPS & CONDIMENTS

Introduction   127

♥ Fat Free

* fat free if using fat free soy milk

SAUCES, DIPS & CONDIMENTS

What provides variety to a vegetarian's diet? Why, a sauce, of course. Any fruit, vegetable or grain can be bathed, dipped, and dressed to dazzle the diner with an endless parade of sensations. A new and exciting sauce can awaken tiresome tastebuds and bring adventure to the table.

Many people pass on sauces due to their high fat and calorie rich ingredients, so we have provided some healthy recipes that will spring board your imagination into future sauce serendipity.

Chile Roja Enchilada Sauce

Roasted ancho or pasilla chiles, create a great and memorable sauce. We learned to make this from the Mexi-Indians in Baja. This is our own adaptation (they use much more oil).

2-3 oz pk	Pasilla chiles, dried (they should be big and ruby black)
2¼ c	Filtered water
1½ tsp	Oregano
2 tsp	Cumin
1 sm can	Tomato paste
1/2 tsp	Sea salt
1	Garlic clove, pressed

1) Bake the chiles in an oven preheated to 350° for 3-4 minutes. Let the chiles cool.
2) Remove the pithy insides, stems, and seeds from the chiles.
3) Put the chiles into a small pan, cover with filtered water, bring to a boil, then simmer on low 15 minutes. Scrape the chile pulp away from its skin using a spoon or butter knife.
4) Put the chile pulp into a blender along with filtered water and blend. Add the other ingredients, continue blending until a smooth texture is obtained.

Yields 4 cups—can be frozen. Besides enchiladas, you can add this sauce to rice or beans for a great flavor.

Note: for less "chile" taste, add extra tomato juice to the recipe (1/2 to 1 cup).

Chile Verde Sauce

This delicious thick green sauce has a distinctive mellow and nutty flavor with a hot after taste.

1/2 c	Almonds
8 lg	Green California chiles (or 1½ cups cooked chiles)
1 med	Onion, chopped
1 sm	Jalapeño, minced and seeded
2	Garlic cloves
2 c	Filtered water
2 Tbl	Cilantro
2 Tbl	Liquid aminos

1) Toast the almonds until lightly browned.
2) Toast the chiles whole in an oven until fragrant and both sides are blistered. Place the chiles into a plastic bag and let them cool, then seed* and skin them.
3) Sauté the onion and jalapeños in liquid aminos until tender, about 5 minutes. Stir occasionally.
4) Put the almonds, chiles, and the rest of the ingredients into a food processor or blender and puree until smooth.
5) Pour the sauce into a saucepan and simmer for 10 minutes.

*Serve with **Chile Verde Enchiladas** (page 251), **Tomatillo Enchilada Casserole** (page 253), **Tofu Chilaquiles** (page 43). Or sauté tofu or tempeh slices in this sauce as a main dish and serve over rice, with beans and tortillas, or serve over pasta. Also delicious over burritos and baked.*

*Note, the sauce will be rather spicy hot if all the seeds are not removed.

Tomato Vegetable Cream Sauce

A heavenly sauce, serve over tortellinis or pasta of your choice.

1/2 c each	Onion, carrot and celery
3 Tbl	White wine
2½ c	Italian tomatoes with juice, chopped
6 lg	Basil leaves, freshly chopped
1 tsp	Vegetable salt substitute
1/2 c	Soy milk
1/4 tsp	Cracked pepper

1) Mince the vegetables in a food processor.
2) Sauté them in wine in a large skillet for a couple of minutes.
3) Add the tomatoes, basil and spices, simmer for 45 minutes stirring now and then with a wooden spoon.
4) Purée the vegetables in a food processor or blender.
5) Transfer the sauce back to the skillet and heat up on medium. Add soy milk and stir until blended, serve over pasta.

Makes about 3½ cups

Mushroom Gravy

Very easy and full of flavor.

1	Garlic clove, pressed
1/2 Tbl	Liquid aminos
1 pkg	Natural mushroom soup mix
1¼ c	Soy milk, or Fat Free Soy Moo
1/4 c	Wine
	Filtered water as needed

1) In a small saucepan, sauté the garlic in the liquid aminos for 3-4 minutes.
2) Add the rest of the ingredients, stir well with a whisk until bubbling. Reduce heat, then simmer 10-15 minutes, stir occasionally.

Yields about 1¾ cups

Eggplant Sauce

This is much more interesting than a typical marinara sauce, serve with fresh pasta, and a large crisp salad.

1	Eggplant
1	Onion
2	Garlic cloves
1/4 c	Red wine
28 oz can	Tomatoes, crushed
6 oz can	Tomato paste and filtered water to thin
1 tsp (each)	Oregano and basil
1/2 tsp (each)	Crushed red pepper and fennel seeds
1/2 tsp	Sea salt
1 Tbl	Lemon juice or 1 lemon wedge
1 Tbl	Honey

1) Skin and dice the eggplant, chop the onion.
2) Press the garlic into the red wine and sauté the garlic in a deep skillet.
3) Add the eggplant and onion, continue stirring for 5 minutes or so.
4) Add tomatoes, paste, water and rest of ingredients.
5) Cook on low heat, covered for 1½ hours. Stir occasionally.

For a meaty sauce add:
Crumbled tempeh marinated in 1 Tbl liquid aminos for 1 hour. Broil until crispy or sauté in a bit of olive oil. Then add the tempeh to the sauce.

Spinach Mint Sauce

A spicy green sauce for grains and vegetables.

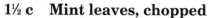

1½ c	Mint leaves, chopped
3	Garlic cloves, peeled and minced
1/2	Serrano chile (seeded), minced
1 Tbl	Lemon juice
1/4 c	Filtered water
5 oz	Spinach, steamed (fresh or frozen)
1 Tbl	Soy milk
1 Tbl	Liquid aminos
	Filtered water to thin, about 3/4 cup

1) Sauté the mint, garlic, and chile in the lemon juice and 1/4 cup of filtered water for 5 minutes.
2) Transfer the sauté to a blender and add the steamed spinach, soy milk, liquid aminos, and filtered water to thin (note, for a creamier sauce use soy milk instead of filtered water).
3) Blend until creamy.

Spinach Tomato Sauce

A simple savory sauce of fresh puréed vegetables.
Serve over pasta.

3	Tomatoes, seeded and chopped
1/2	Onion, chopped
1 bunch	Spinach, ends trimmed and chopped
1/4 c	Filtered water
1 Tbl	Lemon juice
2	Garlic cloves, pressed
1/4 tsp each	Red pepper flakes and nutmeg
1 Tbl	Liquid aminos
1 tsp	Honey

1) Sauté the first three ingredients in the filtered water until tender (about 10 minutes).
2) Purée veggies in a food processor or blender.
3) Add the remaining ingredients to the blender, and blend again.
4) Transfer the sauce to a saucepan and heat it gently before serving. Add soy milk for a thicker sauce.

Tofu Creme Sauce

This is a simple sauce and is tasty on steamed broccoli or other vegetables. Like all basic sauces, you can add various ingredients to suit your taste; try onion, garlic, ginger, or use tomato juice instead of the filtered water. Use it as a type of "sour cream" topping.

1/4 c	Filtered water
1½ tsp	Tamari
1 c	Silken "Lite" tofu, mashed
2½ Tbl	Lemon juice
2 tsp	Fructose or honey
a dash of	Cayenne, black pepper, and nutmeg

Blend until creamy, yields 1¾ cups of sauce.

Light Lemon Sauce

A silky low calorie lemon sauce that resembles drawn butter, yet there is no dairy or fat in it. Excellent over asparagus, broccoli, or artichokes.

2 c	Vegetable broth, or stock
1½ Tbl	Arrowroot powder
1/4 c	Lemon juice and some grated rind if it's organic
1/4 tsp	Turmeric
2 Tbl	Liquid aminos
2	Garlic cloves, pressed
1/2 tsp	Fructose (or honey)
1½ Tbl	Nutritional yeast
	Black pepper or cayenne to taste

1) Heat the broth in a heavy pot.
2) Mix the arrowroot with some cold filtered water and add it to the broth.
3) Add the rest of the ingredients, stirring continuously until the sauce thickens.
4) Serve warm. Adjust the seasonings to taste.

Yields about 2 cups

Pinenut Bechamel Sauce

This is a delicious sauce. Pour over veggies, rice, pasta, or use in casseroles. Use "lite" tofu and fat free soy milk for reduced fat.

1/2 c	Pinenuts
1/4 c	Sunflower seeds
2/3 c	Onion, chopped
3	Garlic cloves, pressed
1 Tbl	Red wine
1 Tbl	Filtered water
1 pkg	Silken "Lite" tofu (10 oz)
1 c	Soy Milk
2 tsp	Lemon juice
1 Tbl	Liquid aminos (or dash of sea salt)
	Saffron (a few grains)
1/2 tsp	Fennel seeds (crushed in a mortar)
1 tsp	Coriander powder
	Cayenne (a dash)

1) Toast the pinenuts and sunflower seeds until golden. Reserve 1 Tbl seeds for garnish.
2) Sauté the chopped onion and garlic cloves in the red wine and filtered water mixture, until onions are transparent.
3) Put the nuts, onion mixture, tofu and the rest of the ingredients into a blender and purée well.
4) Pour the sauce into a saucepan and heat gently before serving.

Makes about 3 cups

Cashew Pepper Gravy

A hearty roasted flavor pervades this creamy oil-less, dairy-less gravy.
Serve over baked potatoes, vegetables and grains.

1	Onion, chopped
1	Lemon, juiced (1/4 cup)
1/2 c	Cashew pieces
2 tsp	Arrowroot powder
2¼ c	Filtered water mixed with;
1 Tbl	Mineral Bouillon (Dr. Bronners)
1 tsp	Onion powder
2 Tbl	Nutritional yeast
1 tsp	Jalapeño, roasted and diced
a pinch of	Cracked black pepper and nutmeg (to taste)

1) Sauté the onion in the lemon juice until tender on low heat.
2) Toast the cashews in the oven until light brown, toast the jalapeño pepper until its skin bubbles.
3) Peel, seed and chop the jalapeño. Put it into a blender or food processor with the nuts and onion and some filtered water—purée.
4) Mix the arrowroot with 1/4 cup of filtered water. Put this mixture into a saucepan and heat up with the remaining ingredients. Stir on simmer until the sauce thickens. Adjust spices to taste.

Garnish with grated lemon peel.

Makes about 2⅔ cups

Toasted Pecan Sauce

A roasted nutty gravy that suits steamed vegetables or noodles.

1/2 c	**Pecans**
1 pk	**Silken "Lite" tofu (10.5 oz)**
1	**Onion**
1	**Celery rib and leaves**
1 Tbl	**Cooking sherry**
1 Tbl	**Lemon juice**
1	**Garlic clove**
	Several parsley sprigs
	Tamari to taste
	Filtered water to thin

1) Toast the pecans lightly, then put them into a food processor and grind them finely, add the tofu, and purée again.
2) Chop the vegetables, heat the lemon juice and sherry in a heavy skillet, then add the vegetables. Stir on low heat, until the vegetables soften.
3) Add the veggies, garlic, parsley and liquids to a food processor, purée until smooth, adding filtered water or broth to desired consistency.
4) Transfer to a medium pot and heat gently before serving.

Makes about 2 cups

Tofu Thai Peanut Sauce

*Serve as a sauce over soba noodles or as a dip for broiled tempeh,
eggrolls, rice or steamed vegetables.*

1 c	Silken "Lite" tofu
3 Tbl	Peanut butter
1 lg	Garlic clove, chopped
1 Tbl	Ginger, skinned, freshly chopped
1 Tbl each	Lime juice and tamari
1	Green onion, chopped
1 Tbl each	Mint and cilantro leaves, chopped
dash of	Red chile flakes
1/3 to 1/2 c	Filtered water

Blend in a blender until smooth,
then refrigerate.

Makes 1¾ cup

Indian Coconut Sauce

*A sensational sweet sauce that can be used as a basis for a
"sweet 'n' sour" sauce—just add chopped pineapple and bell pepper,
and add a dash of cayenne pepper.*

1 c	"Lite" soy milk
2 Tbl	Coconut, shredded
1 Tbl	Peanut butter
1 Tbl	Ginger, skinned and minced
1 tsp	Master Curry (page 156)
1/2 c	Pineapple juice
1/2 tsp	Turmeric (for a nice golden color)
2 tsp	Arrowroot powder

1) Blend all of the ingredients in a blender.
2) Pour the same into a small saucepan and stir with a whisk
   as the sauce thickens on a medium flame. This takes just a
   couple minutes. Serve over grains or vegetables.

Makes 1⅔ cup

Satin Sauce

*A gently spiced serene sauce with hints of orange, apricot
and cardamon. Fresh spices are the key to a rich flavor.*

1 c	**Silken "Lite" tofu**
2 c	**Filtered water**
4 tsp	**Arrowroot**
2 Tbl	**Liquid aminos**
1 Tbl	**Onion powder**
1/2 c	**Orange juice, fresh squeezed**
3/4 tsp each	**Cardamon and nutmeg**
2	**Garlic cloves, chopped**
2 Tbl	**Apricot or peach preserves, unsweetened**
2 Tbl	**White wine**
	Dash of curry powder
2 tsp	**Onion powder**

1) Blend all of the ingredients in a blender.
2) Transfer the blended sauce to a medium sized enamel pot
   and heat gently, stir on low heat until thoroughly warm.

Makes 4 cups

Green Sauce

A Peruvian sauce using tofu, fresh mint, garlic and fresh cilantro.
Excellent on steamed veggies, over pasta, or as a dip.

8 oz	Silken "Lite" tofu
1/3 c	Cilantro, chopped
1/4 c	Mint, chopped
4	Garlic cloves, pressed
1 Tbl	Liquid aminos
1/4 c	Filtered water
	Cayenne to taste

Blend all of the ingredients well in a blender. Add filtered water to desired consistency.

Serves 2-4

Sprouted Garbanzo Sauce

Makes a great puréed soup, and a warm sauce for rice and grains.

1 c	Garbanzo beans, dry
1	Bell pepper
1	Onion
3	Garlic cloves
1/2	Lemon juice
1 Tbl	Olive oil
1/4 c	Torn cilantro leaves
	Sea salt and Cayenne to taste

1) Soak the garbanzos overnight in filtered water. Rinse the garbanzos in the mornings and evenings for 2-4 days, until sprouts appear.
2) Put the garbanzos into a pot and cover with filtered water. Bring beans to a boil, then simmer for 20 minutes.
3) Chop the onions and peppers, mince the garlic, and add them to the pot, cook another 30 minutes or until tender.
4) Transfer all of the ingredients to a blender and blend well. (Add more filtered water as needed.)

Wok Glaze

This is a truly great glaze over any vegetable stir-fry.

1 Tbl	Arrowroot, whisked with
	2 Tbl cool filtered water
1/2 c	Pineapple juice
1/4 c	Mirin (cooking sake)
1 Tbl	Tamari
2 lg	Ginger chunks, skinned, (about 1" square)
2	Garlic cloves, pressed
	Orange wedge squeezed in

1) In a small saucepan, heat the arrowroot mixture, stirring 2 minutes.
2) Add the pineapple juice, mirin, tamari and stir until thick—turn off heat.
3) Press the ginger through a garlic press into the pan, add the garlic and the orange squeeze.
4) Heat the glaze slightly before pouring over the woked vegetables.

Add a dash of red chile flakes and toasted sesame seeds over the vegetables.

Makes about 3/4 cup

Curried Peanut Sauce

Great over squash and rice.

1/4 lb	Silken "Lite" Tofu (1/2 cup)
1/4 c	Peanut butter
1/2 tsp	Curry powder
1 tsp	Onion powder
1/2 c	Filtered water (or soy milk for a richer sauce)
1/8 tsp	Cayenne
	Turmeric for extra golden color

Blend in a blender, heat up before serving.

Makes 1¼ cups

Black Bean Sauce

*Try over woked wild mushrooms and roll up in (mu-shu) pancakes,
or over rice or squash.*

1¼ c	Cooked black beans
3	Garlic cloves, chopped
1 Tbl	Ginger root, skinned and chopped (fresh)
2 Tbl	Liquid aminos
1/2 Tbl	Rice vinegar
1/3 c	Filtered water or stock
	Cayenne to taste

Puree in a blender.

*For a heartier taste stir in 1/4 cup shredded soy cheese and heat
before serving. Garnish with minced chives.*

Meximato Sauce

*Serve over **Chile Rellenos** (page 255) or any other dish longing
for a nicely spiced red sauce.*

1	Tomato, seeded and chopped
1/4	Onion, chopped
1/2	Lemon, juiced
1	Garlic clove, minced
1 (8 oz) can	Tomato sauce
1/2 tsp each	Oregano, cumin and chili powder

1) Sauté the tomatoes, onions, and garlic in the lemon juice on low.
2) Stir constantly, add a little filtered water or broth if necessary.
3) Stir in the tomato sauce and simmer with spices 15 minutes or so.

Makes 1½ cups

≥ Cactus Salsa ≥

A medium-hot versatile green sauce, good hot or cold. Makes a unique gift. Many of its ingredients are found at farmers markets or in the Mexican section at the grocers.

1	Onion, chopped
2 c	Cactus, chopped
1½ c	Tomatillos, chopped
1	Lemon, juiced
7	Anaheim Chiles
3	Jalapeño peppers
2	Garlic cloves, chopped
1 c	Filtered water
1 c	Cilantro leaves
1/2 Tbl	Arrowroot powder (mixed with a bit of filtered water)
2 Tbl	Tamari
1 Tbl	Honey
	Cumin to taste

1) Sauté the onion, cactus and tomatillos in the lemon juice until tender.

2) Toast the chiles and jalapeños in an oven until the skin blisters, then seed, peel and chop them. Put the chiles into a food processor with the garlic and the sautéed vegetables, pulse chop until chunky-puréed. Add the rest of the ingredients.

3) Transfer the salsa to a pot and heat gently, stirring often for 10-15 minutes.

Keep refrigerated.

*Serve with **No-Oil Chips and Salsa** (page 122), Burritos, enchiladas, appetizer platters; or on **Tofu Chilaquiles** (page 43) or **Sunday Scrambler** (page 40).*

Salsa Fresca

Serve with tortilla chips or as a condiment with all sorts of foods.

9-12	Tomatoes
1/2	Red onion
1/2	Yellow onion
4	Jalapeños, seeded
1 c	Cilantro leaves
2 Tbl	Vinegar
4	Garlic cloves
1/2 tsp	Sea salt
1/2 tsp	Cumin powder

1) Seed and chop the tomatoes, finely chop the onions and cilantro. Mince the jalapeños and put them all into a bowl.
2) Add the other ingredients, toss and chill.

Note: *wear rubber gloves while handling the jalapeños or they will burn your fingers.*

Pineapple Salsa

A delightful tropical salsa, serve over broiled tempeh or tofu.

2 c	Pineapple chunks
1/2 c	Onion, minced
1/4 c	Cilantro leaves
1/2	Lemon, juiced
2	Jalapeños, seeded
1	Garlic clove, pressed
2 Tbl	Pimentos
1 tsp	Oregano

1) Press the garlic and 1 jalapeño through a garlic press, thinly slice the second jalapeño.
2) Put all of the ingredients into a medium bowl, toss.

Spicy Cilantro Dipping Sauce

*A thin and spicy sauce perfect for dipping mochi puffs, rice balls
or on any grain that yearns for a jazzy companion.*

2 Tbl	Tamari
1 Tbl	Mirin (cooking sake)
1/4 c	Rice vinegar
1 Tbl	Fresh cilantro leaves, torn, loose pack
1/4 tsp	Red chile flakes
1/2 tsp	Fresh ginger, skinned and minced
1/2 tsp	Jalapeño pepper, minced

Stir all of the ingredients together, refrigerate.

Makes 1/2 cup

Party Black Bean Dip

The melted soy cheese gives these beans an extra creaminess.
However, omit the soy cheese for a fat-free dip.

2 c	Cooked black beans
1 c	Grated Soy jalapeño cheese
2	Garlic cloves, pressed
4	Green onions, minced
1/2 tsp	Sea salt
2 tsp	Cumin
	Dash of cayenne
	Garnish with cilantro leaves

Stir well, serve warm with **No-oil Chips and Salsa** (page 122).

Serves 6

Hummus

16 oz can	Garbanzo beans (2 cups cooked)
1/4 c	Parsley, freshly chopped
2 Tbl	Olive oil or tahini
3	Garlic cloves, pressed
1/4 c	Filtered water (or as needed)
1/4 c	Lemon, juiced
1 tsp	Liquid aminos
	Cracked pepper to taste
	Paprika as garnish

Blend all of the ingredients until smooth, stopping the blender and stirring a few times if necessary.

Serve in a pretty bowl with thin lemon slivers, parsley, paprika sprinkles, and, of course, warmed pita triangles.

Makes 2 cups

Tofu Basil Dip

10.5 oz pack	Silken "Lite" tofu
2 lg	Garlic cloves, chopped
1/4	Red onion, chopped
2	Basil sprigs (leaves only)
1	Tomato, seeded and chopped
1 Tbl	Onion powder
1	Lemon or lime juiced (about 3 Tbl)
1 Tbl	Liquid aminos
	Cayenne

Blend all of the ingredients until smooth and creamy, add filtered water if necessary.

Zucchini Dip

2 c	Chopped zucchinis, steamed until tender
2	Garlic cloves
1	Jalapeño pepper
1 Tbl	Tofu Mayo (page 150)
1/2 tsp each	Coriander powder and tamari
1/2	Avocado
1 tsp	Onion powder

1) Put the zucchinis in a food processor or a blender.
2) Press the garlic and jalapeño through a garlic press.
3) Blend in the rest of the ingredients—chill.

Red Onion Pickles

Sweet, pink, and crunchy, the marinade softens the bite of the onion and makes for a nice condiment.

3	Red onions, peeled and thinly sliced
1/2 c	Lemon juice

Mix together and refrigerate overnight.

Silken Veggie Dip

A low calorie, high protein all purpose dip for vegetables, as a salad topping or alternative to "hummus." This has a crunch from peanuts and chopped veggies along with a spicyness from the garlic and the ginger.

10.5 oz	Silken "Lite" tofu, firm
1/2	Carrot
1/2	Sour pickle
2	Garlic cloves
1 tsp each	Ginger juice, liquid aminos, lemon juice
1 Tbl	Roasted peanuts
	Dash of curry, coriander, cayenne, onion powders

1) Pulse chop the veggies in a food processor, scrape down the sides.
2) Add the tofu and the spices, pulse chop just until blended.

Sprinkle gomasio, cayenne or peanuts on as a garnish.

Pesto

2 c	Freshly torn basil leaves
1/3 c	Olive oil, cold pressed extra virgin
3 Tbl	Pine nuts, toasted lightly
2	Garlic cloves, chopped
1/2 c	Soy Parmesan cheese
1/2 tsp	Sea salt

1) Put all of the ingredients in a blender except the soy cheese, blend until smooth.
2) Stir the soy cheese in by hand for an interesting texture. This can be kept frozen for several months.

Tofu Pecan Paté

Also wonderful as a vegetable dip, simply add more water.

1	Handful of parsley
1/2 c	Soft "Lite" tofu
1 c	Pecans
1/2	Onion, chopped
1	Garlic clove, pressed
1 Tbl	Kuzu, dissolved in 1 Tbl cold filtered water
2 tsp each	Cider vinegar and soy sauce
	Cayenne
1/2 Tbl	Hot filtered water (if necessary)

1) Toast the pecans in a broiler until golden brown.
2) Put them in a food processor, finely grind. Add the tofu and the rest of the ingredients. Stop and scrape down the sides, continue until a smooth puree forms.
3) Put the paté into a small oiled glass bowl, refrigerate.

A Silken Sour Cream-less

A sour cream substitute.

10.5 oz pk	Silken "Lite" tofu
2 Tbl	Lemon juice
1 Tbl	Honey or barley malt syrup

Blend until smooth.

Tofu Mayo

A low calorie mayonnaise substitute. Yields 1 cup of delicious homemade mayo, use it everywhere you would use mayonnaise— on sandwiches and as a base for dips and dressings.

1 c	Silken "Lite" tofu (1/2 lb)
1 tsp	Tarragon or dijon mustard
1 Tbl	Vinegar of choice
1 Tbl	Lemon juice
1/4 tsp	Sea salt or vegetable salt (to taste)

Put all of the ingredients into a blender. Blend or liquefy until silken.

You can vary the flavor by adding fresh minced herbs, garlic, lemon peel and pepper, enjoy!

Makes 1 cup (12, 1 Tbl servings with only 1.6 calories of fat per serving!)

Seed Cheese

A biogenic sunflower cheese that is high in vitamins and enzymes; easy to make and digest. Add fresh minced herbs, onion, garlic and liquid aminos for a real treat. Use to stuff mushrooms, celery ribs, or cherry tomatoes, or as a spread on crackers. Blend with herbs and veggies for salad dressings.

1/2 c   Sunflower seeds (or almonds, cashews or mixture thereof)
1 c   Filtered water

1) Put the seeds into a glass jar, cover with filtered water and let them soak overnight. Rinse and drain away the soak filtered water before putting the seeds into a blender.
2) Blend the seeds and the 1 cup of filtered water in a blender until creamy (add a garlic clove if you wish), transfer the seed sauce back to the jar.
3) Cover and let sit in a warm place (or in a pan of hot water) for 5-9 hours until separation occurs.
4) To serve: Spoon out the soft cheese part on top, store in small container, refrigerate. Or pour the mixture through a cheese cloth (twist tightly and let all of the filtered water drain out), let the seed cheese hang over a bowl for a day for a firm cheese.

Spice and season as desired.

Cucumbermint Raita

A fragrant cooler for well spiced foods.

1/2	Cucumber
1 pt	Soy yogurt, plain
1 c	Cilantro or watercress leaves
1/2 c	Mint leaves
1	Garlic clove, pressed
1 Tbl	Lemon juice
1 tsp	Vegetable salt
	Dash of cayenne

1) Skin and seed the cucumber, shred or dice the flesh.
2) Finely mince the herbs.
3) Stir all of the ingredients together and then chill.

Fig Chutney

This spicy chutney makes a nice gift. Be prepared to preserve it in small glass canning jars afterwards, or freeze it.

30	**figs, fresh (about 5-6 cups)**
1/2 c	**Raisins**
1/4 c	**Ginger, skinned and freshly chopped**
1/4 c	**Lemon juice**
2 med	**Onions, chopped**
1 tsp each	**Cardamon powder, cinnamon and cayenne**
1/2 tsp each	**Clove, nutmeg, coriander, ground**
1/4 c	**Honey**
1 Tbl	**Cider vinegar**
2 tsp	**Agar flakes dissolved into 1 Tbl filtered water**

1) Wash, stem and chop the figs.
2) Put the figs in a heavy cast iron pot, heat on medium, then add the onions, raisins and spices (except the ginger).
3) Put the ginger and lemon juice in a blender and liquefy—strain the ginger juice over the figs in the pot. Add the agar mixture.
4) Stir, cover and cook on low for about 1/2 hour.

Cajun Spice

*Use for **Bon Temp Tofu Creole** (page 247), or in the
Blackened Tofu recipe (page 248), for great results.*

1-3 tsp	Cayenne (mild, medium, hot)
1½ tsp	Black pepper, freshly ground
1½ tsp	Sea salt
2 tsp each	Oregano, thyme, fennel, cumin, cardamon, garlic powder, chile powder and coriander.

Whirl the spices in a blender, or mix all of the ingredients
together by hand. Store in a glass jar, away from heat and light.

Makes 2/3 cup

Dill Delight

1/4 c	Dill weed
1/8 c	Onion powder
2 Tbl	Sesame seeds, toasted
1/4 tsp	Sea salt
	Dash of cayenne

1) Crush the sesame seeds in a nut mill or a grinder, then add
the rest of the herbs.
2) Store the mixture in a shaker jar.

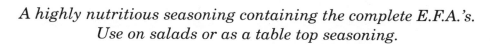

Gomasio of the Sea

A highly nutritious seasoning containing the complete E.F.A.'s.
Use on salads or as a table top seasoning.

2 sheets	Toasted sushi nori
1/2 c	Pumpkin seeds
1/2 c	Flax seeds

1) Gently toast the nori until it's still green, takes only seconds.
2) Grind the seeds in a grinder or nut mill, add the nori.
3) Put the Gomasio into an airtight container and keep refrigerated.

Spicy Sesame Gomasio

A great source of linoleic and linolenic fatty acids (the essential
fatty acids). Use as a garnish over cooked foods or salads.

1/2 c	Flax seeds
1/4 c	Sesame seeds
1/4 c	Pumpkin seeds
1 Tbl	Onion powder
2 tsp	Chile powder blend
1/8 tsp	Sea salt and dash of cayenne

1) Grind the seeds in a nut mill, then put them into a small bowl. Add the rest of the ingredients to the bowl, toss well.
2) Store the gomasio in an airtight container and keep refrigerated to preserve the freshness of the oils.

Note: you can use walnuts, sunflower seeds, and nutritional yeast for other gomasio combinations. Experiment! Enjoy on salads and other dishes.

Master Curry

A fresh and fragrant curry powder, visit your local herb shop or Indian market for available spices.

1/2 c	**Coriander seeds**
10	**Dry red chile pods (without seeds for a milder spice)**
1½ tsp each	**Mustard seeds, fenugreek seeds and black peppercorns**
1 tsp	**Cumin seeds**
15-20	**Curry leaves**
3 Tbl	**Turmeric powder**

1) Using a nut mill or grinder, grind the larger seeds and pods first, then add the powdered spices.
2) Store in glass jars away from the light.

Garam Masala

A traditional spice blend in India that is fun to make, yielding a very unique seasoning.

1/4 c each	**Cumin and coriander seeds**
1½ Tbl	**Cardamon seeds**
2	**Cinnamon sticks, whole 3" long**
1½ tsp	**Whole cloves**
3 Tbl	**Black peppercorns**
4	**Bay leaves**

1) Stir all of the ingredients in a medium hot skillet for 1-2 minutes. Don't let anything burn.
2) Cool the spices, then blend or grind them in a food mill.
3) Store the masala in a light-proof container.

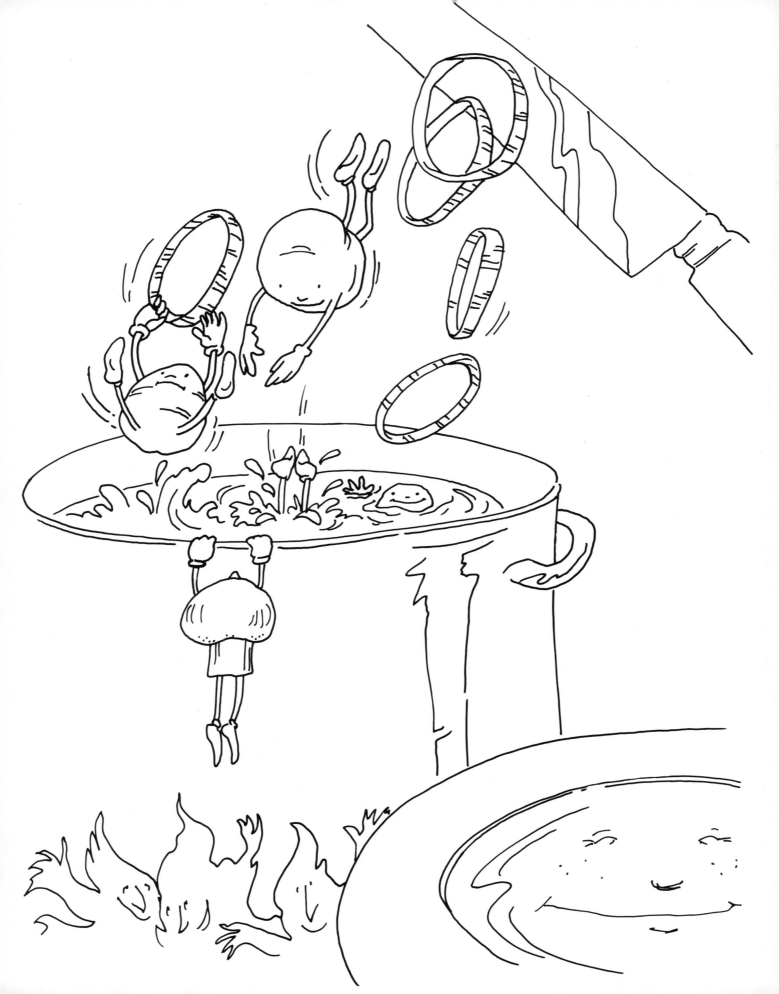

SOUPS

Purifying = Simple soups using vegetables only, very healing and easy to digest.
Creamy = Soups with a soymilk base.
Hearty = soups fortified with tofu, grain or beans.

♥ Fat Free
* fat free if using fat free tofu hot dogs/fat free soy milk

SOUPS

We are very fond of soup. Soup is a symphony, each ingredient singing its own song of life. We like letting time do the cooking. On chilly mornings we'll orchestrate a souphonic event, bring it to a near boil, cover and let it sit without a flame until dusk. It can be so heavenly to return home to a pot of soup, its aroma deliciously melting into the atmosphere, peacefully welcoming us home.

Ah, the seduction of soup. If only people could learn from a vegetables acceptance of being in a pot with many different fellows, yielding into one perfect gift. They give of themselves for the greater taste. Imagine a world where everyone contributes for the betterment of all. What a flavor that would be!

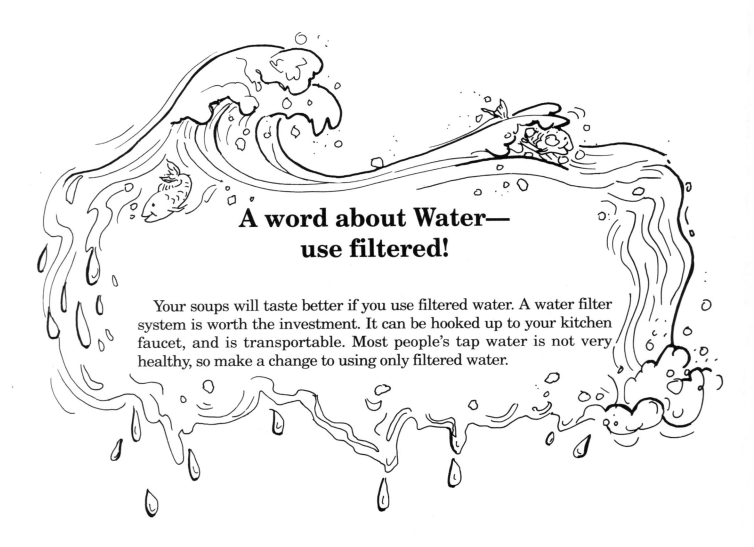

A word about Water— use filtered!

Your soups will taste better if you use filtered water. A water filter system is worth the investment. It can be hooked up to your kitchen faucet, and is transportable. Most people's tap water is not very healthy, so make a change to using only filtered water.

Simple Stock

Prepare the night before.

1	Pot of filtered water (2 quarts)
3 c	Greens, packed (Beet, chard, etc.)
1	Carrot top and leaves
1 c	Fresh parsley
1	Onion, peeled and chopped

1) Bring the water to a boil, add the vegetables, then simmer them for 15-30 minutes on low.
2) Turn the heat off and keep the stock covered overnight.
3) Strain broth in the morning (discard the vegetables).

Reducing Soup

Great hot or cold, may be used as cleansing fast for a couple of days or to assist in weight reduction.

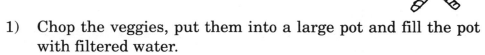

56 oz	Tomatoes, crushed (2 large size cans)
28 oz	Filtered water
1/4 head	Green cabbage
1 head	Red cabbage
1 bunch	Celery
1	Onion
5	Garlic cloves
	Fresh or dried dill to taste

1) Chop the veggies, put them into a large pot and fill the pot with filtered water.
2) Cover the pot and bring it to a near boil, simmer on low for 30 minutes or until vegetables are tender. Store the extra soup in the refrigerator.

Miso Soup

Simple and satisfying.

1 qt	Kombu broth (Dashi)
1/2	Onion, peeled and chopped
1/2 c	Miso, mild yellow
2 Tbl	Red miso
1/2 c	Firm tofu
2 Tbl	Scallions, minced

1) Prepare dashi according to recipe below.
2) Mix the miso in some filtered water until a paste forms.
3) Add the miso to the broth, stir, add the onions and tofu—heat until the onion is tender.

Serve with a garnish of lemon slivers.

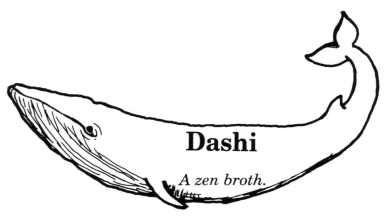

Dashi

A zen broth.

1 qt	Filtered water
1 piece	Kombu (see page 15)
2 tsp	Tamari
	Chopped scallions and cilantro as garnish

1) Rinse the kombu and wipe it dry.
2) Put the kombu into the water and heat for 15 minutes until almost boiling.
3) Add the tamari to taste. Serve with a garnish of tiny cubes of tofu.

Purifying Purees

*Pureed vegetables blended with a bit of seasoning makes
for a simple, easy to digest, cleansing meal.*

Spinach Puree

1 lb	Spinach (frozen ok), chopped
1	Onion, peeled and chopped
1	Garlic clove, pressed
2 Tbl	Lemon juice
2 c	Simple Stock (page 161)
1 Tbl	Liquid aminos
2 Tbl	Nutritional yeast
1/2 tsp	Dill delight

1) Cook the first three ingredients in 1/2 cup of filtered water
   until they are tender, for 10-15 minutes.
2) Put the veggies into a blender and puree one batch at a time.
3) Return the veggie puree to the pot—add the simple stock, stir
   well, then add the spices and heat until warm. Serve and
   garnish with a lemon twist.

Serves 2

Pea Puree

1 lb	Peas (frozen is easy)
1	Onion, peeled and chopped
1	Garlic clove
2 c	Filtered water
1 Tbl	Liquid aminos
1 Tbl	Lemon juice
	Dash of nutmeg

Follow the Spinach Puree directions.

Serves 2

Tropical Carrot Puree

4 lg	Carrots, chopped
1 lg	Onion, peeled and chopped
2 c	Filtered water
1	Banana, chopped
1	Garlic clove, pressed
1 Tbl	Peanut butter (not so purifying, but delicious)
	Dash of liquid aminos

1) Steam the carrots and onion in filtered water until they are
   tender. Puree the vegetables in a blender or a food processor,
   adding the rest of the ingredients until puree is complete.
2) Gently heat before serving.

Serves 2

Banana Saffron Carrot Puree

A delicately spiced puree with Indonesian flavors—
terrific and good for you.

1/4 c	**White wine or sake**
2 c	**Filtered water**
1½ lbs	**Young carrots, chopped (fresh or frozen)**
1/2	**Banana (about 4")**
1	**Garlic clove, pressed**
1 tsp	**Ginger, fresh, skinned and chopped**
1 Tbl	**Liquid aminos**
1/8 tsp	**Fennel seeds, crushed**
1/8 tsp	**Chile flakes, crushed**
sm. pinch	**Saffron threads, clove powder and wasabi powder**
1/2 tsp	**Curry powder**
	Garnish with cilantro leaves

1) Bring the liquids to a boil, add the carrots and banana, then cover and simmer for 10 minutes.

2) Puree the carrots and banana in a blender, reserving a few carrots in the pot for texture. Add the spices and puree for several seconds.

3) Add the reserved carrots, pulse chop briefly to keep a texture to the puree.

4) Transfer the puree back to the pot and heat gently to meld flavors before serving.

Serves 3-4

Spicy Cilantro Zucchini

A creamy green soup spiced with red chile pulp.

4-5 c	Zucchini
1	Onion, peeled
1	Bell pepper
1/2 bunch	Cilantro, fresh
2 c	Filtered water
1	Red chile, dried (about 5" long)
1/2 tsp	Oregano
1	Garlic clove, pressed
1-2 Tbl	Liquid aminos (to taste)

1) Chop the vegetables, add them to a pot of boiling water and simmer them covered until they are tender. Puree, then transfer the puree back to the pot.

2) Meanwhile, cook the chile in a small pan of boiling filtered water for 10 minutes. Squeeze the chile pulp into the puree.

3) Stir in all of the remaining ingredients, adjust the spices to your taste and serve hot.

Corny Carrot Pepper

A delicious full bodied soup using fresh basil, cumin and sage.

1/2	**Red bell pepper**
1/2	**Yellow bell pepper**
5	**Carrots**
2	**Onions, peeled**
2 c	**Corn, cut (frozen is OK)**
1/2 bunch	**Basil leaves, torn (about 1/2 cup)**
1	**Garlic clove, pressed**
2 Tbl	**Bronner's liquid bouillon**
1/2 tsp	**Cumin and onion powder**
2 Tbl	**Brewers yeast**
Pinch	**Sage**
	Cracked black pepper or cayenne to taste

1) Chop all of the veggies (first 6 items) and then put them into a large soup pot with about 2 cups of filtered water. Bring to a boil, then cover and simmer them for 15 minutes.
2) Transfer the veggies to a blender or a food processor and puree.
3) Return the puree back to the pot, and stir in the rest of the ingredients. Simmer until hot, add filtered water if necessary and adjust the seasoning to your taste.

Mediterranean Puree

2 sm	Eggplants, peeled, chopped
1 bunch	Spinach leaves
1	Onion, peeled and chopped
4	Garlic cloves
1 c	Simple Stock (page 161) or broth
2 Tbl	Lemon juice
3 Tbl	Liquid aminos
1 tsp	Oregano, basil mix or Italian seasoning
1/2 Tbl	Honey
3 Tbl	Nutritional yeast
2 c	Broth or filtered water (as needed)

1) Steam the first 5 ingredients for 20 minutes.
2) Puree in batches in a food processor until smooth, then return to the pot.
3) Heat gently and add the remaining ingredients. Simmer for 20 more minutes.

Puree of Simmered Greens

A delicate and mineral rich puree.

30-40	Beet leaves (fresh tender)
15-20	Swiss (green) chard leaves
2½ c	Simple Stock (page 161)
2	Garlic cloves, pressed
2 tsp	Tamari
1/4 tsp	Ginger, skinned, grated and fresh
	Cut 1/2 cup carrot "flowers" to float in soup (see page 62)

1) Rinse and tear the beet and chard leaves into large pieces. Put the leaves into a pot with Simple Stock. Bring to a boil, simmer for 5-10 minutes until tender (leaves will steam down dramatically in size).
2) Put the greens in a food processor or a blender and puree. Return the puree to cooking pan (into broth that is there), add the rest of the ingredients. Heat gently then serve.

Serves 2-3

Tomato Kale Soup

This is a hearty and delicious soup.

1 qt	Filtered water
1 bunch	Kale
1/4	Red cabbage
1	Potato
1 lg	Carrot
5	Garlic cloves, pressed
28 oz can	Tomatoes, crushed
1/2 tsp	Coriander
1 tsp	Dill or dill delight (*see condiments)
1 Tbl	Onion powder

1) Chop the kale, cabbage, carrot, and cube the potato.
2) Put the veggies into a pot with filtered water, bring to a near boil, then simmer covered for 20 minutes.
3) Add the spices, and simmer for a couple of minutes more.

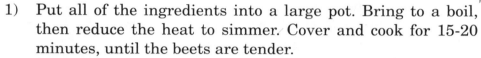

Beet Borscht

8 c	Chopped beets
1 lg	Onion
5	Garlic cloves
2 c	Filtered water
1	Carrot
1/4	Green cabbage
	Cracked pepper and sea salt to taste

1) Put all of the ingredients into a large pot. Bring to a boil, then reduce the heat to simmer. Cover and cook for 15-20 minutes, until the beets are tender.
2) Transfer the vegetables to a food processor or a blender and puree (sections at a time). Returning each pureed batch to the pot.
3) Serve hot or chilled and top with **Silken Sour Cream-less—** (page 150).

Curried Carrot Puree

7 med	Carrots, chopped
2 c	Filtered water
3	Garlic cloves, pressed
1 tsp	Fresh ginger, skinned and grated
1/4 tsp	Cinnamon
1 tsp	Master Curry (page 156)
2 Tbl	Liquid aminos
1 Tbl	Maple syrup or apple concentrate
2 Tbl	Nutritional yeast

1) Steam the carrots in the filtered water for 20 minutes, or until tender
2) Puree the carrots in a food processor or a blender, adding the filtered water from their steaming (usually 2 batches will do).
3) Add the garlic and ginger to the last puree batch.
4) Put the puree back into the pot, add filtered water for desired consistency and the rest of the spices. Heat gently until warm.

Red Chile Zucchini Soup

A rich deep color pervades this chile lovers delight.
Easy to make and good for you.

1	Dried red chile (6" long)
6	Zucchinis, chopped
1	Onion, chopped
2	Garlic cloves
1 c	Filtered water
	Sea salt, cumin and oregano to taste
1 tsp	Liquid aminos or tamari

1) Lightly toast the chile in an oven for 2 minutes.
2) Stem and seed the chile, tear it in half and put it into a large pot with the zucchinis, onion and filtered water. Bring to a boil, then simmer for 15 minutes. Scrape the flesh from the chile skin and add it back to the pot, discard the skin.
3) Puree half of the soup, then return it back to the pan and stir in the rest of the seasoning. Serve warm.

Delicious served with **Green Chile Corn Bread** *(page 214) and* **3-Pepper Black Bean Salad** *(page 81).*

Native Chile Corn Chowder

A quick and easy healthy stew that is a favorite; the chile thickens and provides a rich background flavor.

5	Crook neck yellow squash
1	Bell pepper
1	Carrot
1/2 c	Parsley, packed
1 lg	Dried red chile (6" long)
1 c	Corn, cut
2	Garlic cloves
1/2 tsp	Cumin
	Pinch of cinnamon
1 tsp	Liquid aminos
	Filtered water

1) Lightly toast the chile for 2 minutes, then seed and stem it.
2) Chop the veggies and put them in a pot. Add the chile and 2 cups of filtered water and then cover the pot. Bring to a boil, then turn down the heat to simmer for 10 minutes. Remove the chile, scrape the chile flesh into the pot—discard the skin.
3) Puree these vegetables in a food processor (puree all but a few chunks of squash for texture).
4) Add the corn, garlic and spices, and the filtered water to thin to a desired consistency. Heat gently before serving.

Leek Flower Soup

A thick creamy-like soup that melts in your mouth. Cauliflower and leek flavors are heightened by the garlic and dill, simply divine.

1 lg	Head of cauliflower
1 lg	Leek
5	Garlic cloves
1 c	Beet (or other) greens
4 c	Filtered water
2 Tbl	Liquid aminos
1 Tbl	Nutritional yeast

To taste:	Dill weed
	Onion powder
	Dash of cayenne

1) Chop all of the vegetables. Boil the filtered water in a large soup pot, add the chopped veggies and cook them covered for 10 minutes on low heat.

2) Add the garlic and spices, continue cooking for 5 more minutes, until tender.

3) Puree 1/2 of the soup (all the greens) and then add the puree back to the pot—stir and serve.

Cream Soups—your creation:

Any vegetable can become "creamed" by steaming it, putting it into the blender or the food processor with a bit of soft tofu (silken "Lite" tofu) and or soy milk ("Lite" soy milk), filtered water from steaming and your favorite herbs and spices. This is a non fat version of the calorie—cholesterol laden dairy-based soups, and is terrific! Happy discoveries.

Cream of Sweet Lima Bean

2 c	Lima beans (frozen is easy)
1	Onion, peeled and chopped
1/2 c	"Lite" soy milk (vanilla soy milk adds a nice natural sweetness)
1/2	Fresh serrano chile (the small hot ones)
1 tsp	Liquid aminos
2	Parsley sprigs
1	Marjoram sprig, fresh or oregano (leaves only)
1 c	Filtered water (as needed)

1) Steam or cook the lima beans with the onion until they are tender.
2) Put the vegetables into a blender with the remaining ingredients, adding the filtered water as needed (including the steam water).
3) Serve, or heat gently in a pan to keep warm.

Butternut Creme Soup

A wonderful way to have your squash.

- 1   **Butternut squash (about 2-2½ lbs)**
- 1 c   **Filtered water**
- 1   **Garlic clove, pressed**
- 1/2 Tbl **Liquid aminos**
-      **"Lite" soy milk to thin**
-      **Cayenne and curry powder to taste**

1) Seed the squash and cut it into large chunks. Steam the squash until tender in 1 cup of filtered water. When cool remove the squash skin.
2) Put the squash into a blender with some of the steam filtered water and blend; adding the spices and soymilk to taste.
3) Heat to warm, then serve.

For a really beautiful presentation, serve it in a pumpkin shell:

1) Cut the top off of a pumpkin and hollow it out. (You may use the top as a cover.)
2) Pour the boiling filtered water inside and let it sit for 1 hour.
3) Pour out the filtered water.
4) Fill the pumpkin shell with the hot soup.

Cream of Mushroom

1½ lbs	Mushrooms, fresh
1	Onion, peeled and chopped
5	Garlic cloves
1 c	Celery and leaves
1/2 c each	Filtered water and wine
10.5 oz pk	Silken "Lite" tofu
1 c	"Lite" soy milk
1 Tbl	Onion powder
1/4 c	Liquid aminos

1) Clean the mushrooms with a wet towel, trim and chop them coarsely with the other vegetables.
2) Put the veggies into the filtered water/wine mixture and cook them for 15 minutes, leaving them to simmer on low.
3) Puree the veggies with the tofu, soy milk and spices.
4) Return the puree to the pot and gently heat before serving.

Garnish with minced parsley.

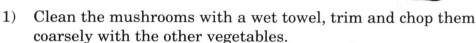

Cream of Gold

A puree of curried golden zucchini and apple.

2 lg	Zucchinis (gold ones)—10-12" long each, 3" diameter
1	Apple, chopped
3/4 c	Broth or "Lite" soy milk
1/2 tsp	Master Curry (page 156)
1½ Tbl	Honey or apple juice concentrate
1/4-1/2 tsp	Cinnamon
1 Tbl	Liquid aminos, or tamari

1) Cut up and steam the zucchinis and apple in 1 cup of filtered water for about 10 minutes.
2) Puree them when tender in a blender or a food processor. Put the puree back into the pot and add the remaining ingredients.

Heat gently before serving.

Spicy Eggplant Creme

2	**Eggplants**
2	**Onions, peeled**
2	**Garlic cloves, pressed**
1/2	**Lemon juiced**
1 c	**Filtered water or broth**
2 c	**"Lite" soy milk**
2 tsp	**Tamari (or 1 Tbl liquid aminos)**
1/2 tsp	**Curry powder**
1/4 tsp each	**Cumin, and oregano**
	Cracked black pepper and cayenne to taste
	Parsley as garnish

1) Slice the eggplants lengthwise. Sprinkle sea salt on top and let them sweat for 10-15 minutes, then blot dry.

2) Bake the eggplants and onions in an oven for 30 minutes, then remove the skin from the eggplants (or steam them both for 15 minutes until tender).

3) Puree the onions and eggplant in a food processor or a blender adding all of the ingredients except the "Lite" soy milk.

4) Transfer the puree to a soup pot and add the "Lite" soy milk, heat gently. Simmer 5 minutes or until thoroughly warm.

Serve with crusty bread or whole grain crackers and a crisp tossed salad.

Thanksgiving Yam

A perfect cream soup for the Holidays, very easy to prepare.
Try substituting sweet potatoes for a less sweet soup.

1 lg	Yam (about 2 cups cooked), chopped
1	Garlic clove, pressed
1 c	Apple cider, naturally spiced
1/3 c	"Lite" vanilla soy milk (or regular for a less sweet taste)
1/2 c	Filtered water (or more to thin)
1/4 tsp	Master Curry (page 156)

1) Cook or steam the yam in a little filtered water until tender. Let it cool, then remove the skin.
2) Put all of the ingredients into a blender and blend them until they are thick, smooth and creamy. Adjust the liquids to suit your personal taste. (More "Lite" soy milk will yield a creamier texture).
3) Heat gently before serving

Garnish with a small flower or leaf—fresh mint or cilantro will do nicely.

Sopa de Ajo

A Spanish garlic soup that works
magic on your vitality!

1/2 c	Garlic, chopped (1 big bulb)
1½ qts	Filtered water
1/4 c	Rice
6" piece	Kombu
1/8 tsp	Cayenne to taste
1 tsp	Olive Oil
1 slice	Wheat bread, toasted, cubed
1 Tbl	Liquid aminos to taste

1) Prepare the stock by rinsing the kombu and wiping it dry.
2) Bring the filtered water to a boil. Add the kombu and rice, reduce heat and simmer for 15-20 minutes, remove the kombu.
3) Heat the olive oil and the liquid aminos in a skillet, add the garlic, sauté lightly, then add the bread cubes. After a couple of minutes transfer 1/2 cup of kombu broth into the skillet, then transfer it all back into the large pot.
4) Stir gently and serve hot!

Rosey Vegetable

A hearty vegetable soup with a gorgeous ruby color.

2½ qts	Simple stock (page 161)
1/2 c	Barley, rinsed
3	Red potatoes, chopped
2 c	Celery, minced
2	Beets, chopped
1 c	Packed greens, chopped
1	Red onion, peeled and sliced
1/2 tsp	Red chile flakes, dried
1 Tbl each	Lemon juice, coriander and tamari
1/2 Tbl	Sweet basil
1 tsp each	Dill, cumin and onion powder
1/4 c	Liquid aminos
2	Garlic cloves, pressed

1) Bring the stock to a boil, add the washed barley. Cover and simmer for 15 minutes.

2) Add all of the remaining veggies to the pot along with the spices—simmer an hour or so.

Asian Carrot Soup

*A delicate soup that melts in your mouth
with a first impression of wow!*

1/2	**Onion, peeled and chopped**
1/2 Tbl	**Olive oil**
2 Tbl	**Sake**
4 lg	**Garlic cloves, pressed**
4-5 lg	**Carrots, shredded**
3	**Zucchinis, shredded**
2 Tbl	**Miso**
2 Tbl	**Peanut butter**

1) Sauté the onion on medium high heat in the olive oil and sake, add the garlic after a few minutes. Stir well, reduce heat to a simmer.

2) Add the carrots to the pot, stir well, then put in the zucchinis. Add filtered water to just cover then put a lid on the pot. Simmer for 10 minutes.

3) Add the miso and peanut butter (stir them together first in a little filtered water).

4) Add more filtered water to cover the ingredients, stir well, then cover to simmer 15 more minutes (or until the veggies are just tender).

Serve with a tofu marinade and a fresh green salad for a great color feast.

Southwest Bean Chowder

Chile, wine, lemons and cilantro give punch to this hearty veggie stew.

1½ c	**Dried garbanzos**
1	**Onion, peeled and sliced**
4	**Garlic cloves, minced**
2	**Bay leaves**
3	**Carrots, finely chopped**
1/4 c	**Parsley, finely chopped**
1 Tbl	**Oregano**
1/2 c	**White wine, dry**
1/2	**Lemon juiced, and slice of peel**
16 oz	**Tomatoes, crushed**
2 med	**Zucchinis, sliced in rounds**
1 lg ear	**Corn, shredded**
1/2 tsp	**Vegetable salt**
1 Tbl	**Cumin**
1 tsp	**Chile powder**
1/4 c	**Soy cheese of choice, shredded**
	Cilantro for garnish

1) Rinse the garbanzos and soak them overnight in a pot of filtered water. Bring them to a boil the next morning, turn down to simmer.
2) Add the next 5 ingredients after 15 minutes. Cook for 1/2 hour, covered on low.
3) Add all of the remaining ingredients, and cover, and simmer for 20 more minutes.

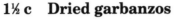

Summer Minestrone

A satisfying minestrone with a nice flavor.

1 c	Garbanzos, white beans or red beans (soak beans overnight in 4 cups of filtered water in a big enamel soup pot)
1 Tbl	Olive oil
5 c	Shredded greens (beet, escarole or chard)
1 c	Zucchinis, chopped
1/4 c	Garlic, chopped
28 oz	Tomatoes with juice, chopped
1	Lemon slice
bunch	Basil leaves (at least 1/2 cup packed)
1/2 tsp each	Pulverized fennel seeds and red chile flakes
1/2 Tbl	Italian herbs
1/4 c	Wine, dry

1) Bring the filtered water and beans to a boil in the soup pot—reduce the heat, add the olive oil and simmer for 1 hour.
2) Add all of the remaining ingredients and more filtered water to cover. Put the lid on and simmer for 1 more hour, then turn off the heat.

Very good with grated soy parmesan on each serving.

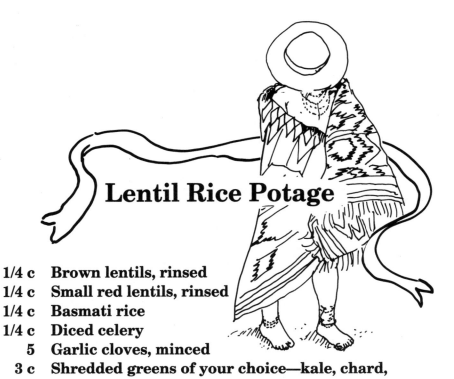

Lentil Rice Potage

1/4 c	Brown lentils, rinsed
1/4 c	Small red lentils, rinsed
1/4 c	Basmati rice
1/4 c	Diced celery
5	Garlic cloves, minced
3 c	Shredded greens of your choice—kale, chard, endive
1	Onion, peeled and chopped
1 Tbl	Onion powder
3 Tbl	Tamari
1/2 Tbl each	Coriander and cumin powder
1 Tbl	Italian herb blend
1 tsp	Crushed red peppers, dried

1) Put the lentils and grains into a large soup pot filled with boiling filtered water, then add the diced celery and garlic.
2) Cook for 15-20 minutes, covered, on low heat.
3) Add the greens and all of the remaining ingredients, simmer on low heat for 1 hour.

Top with gomasio.

Tomato Barley Vegetable

A fragrant satisfying soup with many herbs.

1/2 gallon	**Filtered water**
2 tsp	**Fennel seeds**
1 tsp	**Cumin seeds**
1 tsp	**Thyme**
1/4 tsp	**Dried chile flakes**
1/2 c	**Barley, rinsed**
2 med	**Onions, peeled**
3 c	**Zucchini**
28 oz (can)	**Tomatoes, crushed**
2 c	**Cauliflower**
1/2 c	**Red wine**
1 Tbl	**Liquid aminos or Bronner's**
	Several fresh cilantro leaves and/or oregano leaves

1) Boil the filtered water in a large soup pot.
2) Grind the spices in a blender, set aside.
3) Chop the vegetables.
4) Add the rinsed barley to the soup pot. Then add the veggies and spices. Simmer covered for 15-25 minutes. Add the wine last. Garnish with herbs.

Serves 6

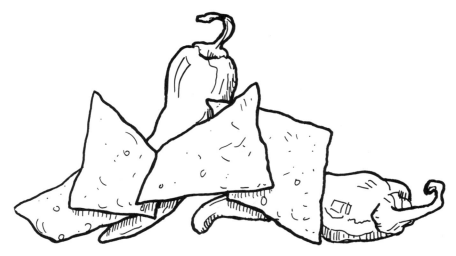

Green Chile Tortilla Soup

In the mood for a fiesta? Try this soup.

2 lg	Zucchinis, chopped coarsely
1	Anaheim green chile, chopped coarsely
1/2 can	Green chiles, roasted, and diced (1/2 lb.)
1 Tbl	Garlic, minced
1/2 c	Cilantro, minced
4	Corn tortillas (or leftover tortilla chips) cut into squares and toasted in an oven briefly
1/4 c	Loose pack fresh oregano leaves (or 2 Tbl dried)
1 Tbl	Vegetable broth seasoning

1) Put all of the ingredients into a large pot—cover with filtered water. Bring pot to a boil, then reduce to simmer. Cook until the vegetables are just soft, about 25 minutes.
2) Add a dash of sea salt or tamari to taste.

Ragin' Cajun Peanut Barley Stew

 A spirited hearty soup.

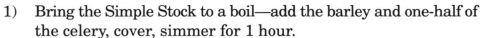

3/4 c	Barley
1 qt	Simple Stock (page 161)
1 c	Celery, diced
2	Carrots, diced
2	Garlic cloves, pressed
1/4	Red cabbage, chopped
2 Tbl	Peanut butter
1/2 c	Peanuts, dry roasted and unsalted
2 Tbl	Dr. Bronner's mineral bouillon
1/4 c	Liquid aminos
28 oz can	Tomatoes, crushed
1 Tbl	Cajun spice (on page 154)
1/2 tsp	Dill salt

1) Bring the Simple Stock to a boil—add the barley and one-half of the celery, cover, simmer for 1 hour.

2) Add the rest of the veggies and spices and simmer for another 1/2 hour.

Petite Orange Lentil Soup

A very fragrant aromatic soup with a luscious color.

1½ qts	Filtered water
1 c	Petite orange lentils (masoor dal)
3 lg	Garlic cloves
1	Onion, peeled and chopped
1" piece	Ginger, skinned and minced
1 tsp each	Turmeric, coriander and tamari
1/2 tsp	Red chile flakes, crushed
16 oz can	Tomato paste
1 tsp	Orange peel gratings
	Dash nutmeg

1) Put the lentils into a pot with the filtered water, bring to a boil and simmer, stirring occasionally.
2) Add the next 6 ingredients. Skim the foam off the top, and cook until tender (1/2 hour or so).
3) Add orange peel and nutmeg and adjust the seasonings to taste.

Serve with Basmati rice and a crisp salad.

Serves 4

Dolphin Paradise

A Pacific sea vegetable-noodle soup featuring tofu and soba
in a sesame miso broth.

3 qts	Filtered water
1 oz	Sea vegetables*, dried
6-10 oz	Soba noodles
1	Onion, peeled and chopped
1	Carrot, minced
1	Zucchini, chopped
6 oz	Firm tofu or 5-spice tofu, cubed
2 Tbl	Miso, mild golden mixed into a paste with water
1 tsp	Fresh ginger, skinned and pressed through garlic press
1 tsp	Chile sesame oil
	Toasted sesame seeds for garnish

1) Bring the filtered water to a boil in a soup pot, cook the sea vegetables for 10 minutes on a medium flame.
2) Meanwhile, pulse chop the veggies in a food processor.
3) Add the soba noodles and onion to the pot, cook until al dente, pull them out and drain them separately.
4) Add the rest of the vegetables to the broth, cook for 10 minutes, then add the noodles and spices, simmer a few moments before serving.

Found in natural food stores.

Tofu Cioppino

1 pk	Tofu, firm, marinated in: 1/2 Tbl lemon juice, 3 garlic cloves, pressed, 1/8 tsp saffron threads, 1 Tbl liquid aminos, sprig of basil
1½ qts	Stock from veggies (onion, garlic, celery tops, bay leaves and peppercorns) or Simple Stock (page 161)
32 oz can	Tomatoes, crushed
2	Onions, peeled and minced
1 c	Potatoes, small cubed
1 lg	Garlic clove, pressed
1/4 c	Red wine
Pinch	Cayenne, cardamom powder and saffron to taste

1) Prepare the tofu a day ahead for the most flavor: Press all of the water out of the firm tofu (lay a towel over it and place a heavy pot on top), cube, then marinate it for 4 hours or more.
2) Simmer the stock for 2 hours, then strain out the vegetables.
3) Add all of the remaining ingredients, simmer for 1 hour or until the potatoes are cooked.
4) Adjust the seasonings to taste.

Serve with a crusty bread and a crisp salad. Garnish with grated soy parmesan cheese and a parsley sprig.

Caldo Natalia

A fragrant Mexican vegetable soup—our favorite—
serve over rice and top with more delicacies.

5	**Anaheim chiles (long green ones)**
3	**Zucchinis**
2 lg	**Carrots**
1 c	**Red onion, peeled**
15 oz can	**Garbanzos**
1/2 tsp	**Ground cloves**
3 Tbl	**Garlic cloves, minced**
1 Tbl each	**Oregano and cumin**
2 Tbl	**Liquid aminos**
1 tsp	**Cracked black pepper**
A few	**Fresh basil sprigs**
1½ qrts	**Simple Stock (page 161)**

1) Slice the chiles lengthwise, remove the seeds and chop; slice the zucchinis and carrots, and chop the onion.

2) Heat up the stock in a large pot, add the vegetables, pressed garlic and spices and heat to boiling. Then quickly reduce to simmer, cover and cook until the vegetables are tender, about 15 minutes. You may also puree half of it for a soup with more body.

3) Serve with **Natalia's Rice** (page 203) and top each serving with a spoonful of each:

> **chopped tomatoes**
> **cilantro**
> **sliced avocados**
> **minced onion**
> **and a shake of soy parmesan**

Cilantro Barley Stew

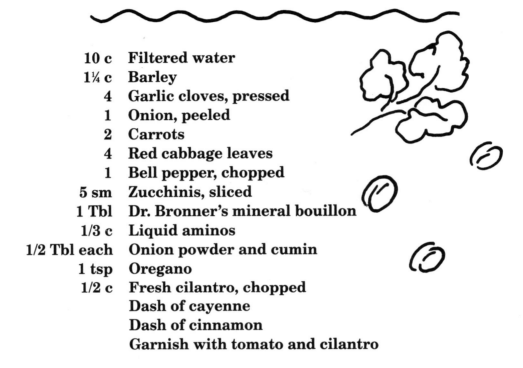

10 c	Filtered water
1¼ c	Barley
4	Garlic cloves, pressed
1	Onion, peeled
2	Carrots
4	Red cabbage leaves
1	Bell pepper, chopped
5 sm	Zucchinis, sliced
1 Tbl	Dr. Bronner's mineral bouillon
1/3 c	Liquid aminos
1/2 Tbl each	Onion powder and cumin
1 tsp	Oregano
1/2 c	Fresh cilantro, chopped
	Dash of cayenne
	Dash of cinnamon
	Garnish with tomato and cilantro

1) Bring the filtered water to a boil.
2) Add the barley and garlic to the water. Return to a boil, turn down heat to simmer, cover and cook for 1/2 hour.
3) Finely chop the onions, carrots and cabbage, slice the zucchini. Add the vegetables and simmer for 1/2 hour more.
4) Add the spices and simmer a few more minutes until all has blossomed!

Top each bowl with 1/4 tomato, seeded and chopped, and a few cilantro leaves.

Couscous Stew

*The spices are many, but create a tapestry of wonderful seasoning,
fragrance and color.*

7-8	Potatoes
6	Carrots
2	Onions, peeled
1/2 bunch	Parsley
1 c	Radishes
3½ qts	Kombu broth*
5 lg	Garlic cloves
5	Cherry tomatoes
1/4 c	Couscous
1/4 c	Tomato paste
1 Tbl each	Onion powder, coriander, basil, dill, cooking sherry and tamari
1 tsp each	Cumin, chili powder, turmeric Ginger, skinned and freshly grated (put through garlic press)
1/2 tsp each	Nutmeg and cardamom Dash cayenne
2 tsp	Arrowroot powder mixed with 1/4 cup filtered water

1) Dice and peel the potatoes, chop the carrots, onions and parsley, quarter the radishes and put them all into a large pot of Kombu broth.
2) Bring the broth to a boil, then turn heat to low, simmer covered for 20 minutes.
3) Stir in all of the remaining ingredients.
4) Heat until warmed throughout (about 15 minutes). Make sure couscous is tender before serving.

Kombu Broth (or see "Dashi" on page 162)
*Bring 3½ qrts of water to a boil, add a piece of rinsed Kombu seaweed and return the filtered water to a boil. Simmer gently for 15 minutes. Strain out the Kombu.

Smoky Lentil Soup

Hearty tofu pup'n lentil stew.

1 Tbl	**Liquid aminos**
1 lg	**Leek, sliced**
1 lg	**Carrot, minced**
3 lg	**Garlic cloves, minced**
1 c	**Washed lentils**
2	**Tofu browners or pups*, chopped**
32 oz can	**Tomatoes, cut**
1 Tbl	**Cumin seeds, crushed or powder**
3 sprigs	**Fresh basil tops**
1/2 tsp	**Chile powder**

1) Sauté the liquid aminos with the leek, carrot, and garlic in a pot—add the browners and lentils, then stir for a few minutes.

2) Add 1 can of peeled stewed tomatoes and their juice. Cover the vegetables with filtered water and bring to a boil, then add the spices.

3) Simmer for 2 hours—or turn the heat off and keep it covered all day. Reheat before serving.

*Tofu hot dogs are found in the refrigerated section of Natural Food Stores. (Non-fat varieties are available!)

193

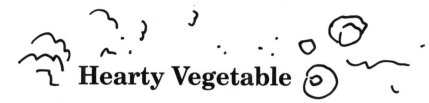

Hearty Vegetable

A meal in itself, begin this in the morning and let it sit
covered without a flame until the evening.

1 lg	Pot of filtered water (about 3 qrts)
1/2 c	Aduki beans
1/2 c	Barley
1/2	Eggplant
2	Carrots
5	Garlic cloves
	Few clusters of parsley
	Few chives
1/2 c	Peas, fresh or frozen
1 tsp each	Turmeric, curry and cumin
1 Tbl each	Coriander, onion and basil (dried)
2 tsp	Dill or dill delight (page 154)
1/4 tsp	Red chile flakes
2	Zucchinis, sliced
1 c	Tomatoes, seeded, chopped
2 Tbl	Dr. Bronner's mineral bouillon

1) Bring the pot of filtered water to a boil, add the beans and barley, continue cooking for 10-15 minutes.
2) Shred the next 5 ingredients in a food processor or chop them fine.
3) Add the vegetables to the pot along with peas and spices. Continue cooking for 1/2 hour covered on low, then turn off the heat and let everything melt into a harmonious ecstasy!
4) Add the sliced zucchinis, chopped tomatoes and seasoning and simmer for 10 minutes before serving.

Chilled Papaya Bisque

A soothing tropical puree with a hint of lime and mint.
A nice prelude of spicey meals.

3 c	**Papaya flesh, chopped**
1/2 c	**Coconut milk (or "Lite" soy milk with 1/2 tsp coconut extract)**
5 Tbl	**Chopped dates, pitted**
1/4 c	**Lime juice, fresh**
1 c	**Filtered water**
1/4 c	**Orange juice**
7	**Mint leaves, chopped**

Blend all of the ingredients until smooth and creamy. Chill before serving, garnish each bowl with a mint leaf.

Serves 4

Chilled Cucumber Soup

A light mint colored icy refresher.

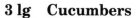

3 lg	**Cucumbers**
6 oz	**Tofu (or "Lite" silken tofu)**
1/2 tsp	**Onion powder**
6-9	**Fresh mint or basil leaves**
1 tsp	**Vegetable salt substitute**
1	**Lemon, juiced**
3/4 c	**Peppermint tea, brewed**
	(Adding "Lite" soy milk or soy yogurt will create a creamy consistency)
	Cracked pepper to taste

1) Peel and chop the cucumbers—seed them too.
2) Puree the cucumbers in batches, in a blender or a food processor. Add all of the remaining ingredients and puree well.
3) Chill before serving. Float a small pink flower or nasturtium on top for a colorful garnish.

Serves 4

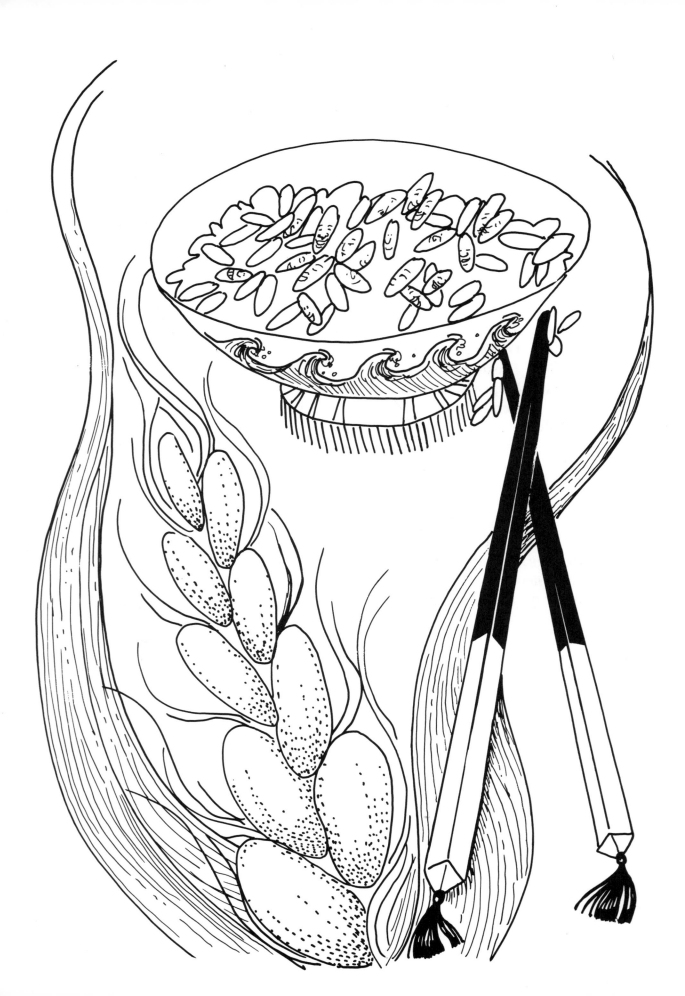

GRAINS, BEANS & BREAD

♥ Fat Free

GRAINS

Ah yes, those delectable carbohydrates few can live without. Grains truly are a staple in vegetarian cooking, and have been a mainstay in all people's diets throughout our global history.

The cultivation of grains represents our working with mother Earth. Since antiquity grains have been found entombed in pyramids and burial chambers.

Whole grains provide valuable nutrition and roughage not obtainable from refined flour products. It is therefore important to consume these "kernels of life" whole, whether sprouted, steamed, sauteed or baked. They are delicious in salads, soups, breads and casseroles or simply by themselves, as in the following recipes.

Brown Rice Crust

A delicious pizza crust made of whole cooked rice and onions.
Use this versatile recipe to make pizza crusts, rice balls, "calzone"
crusts, or quiche crusts. The goodness from whole grains
will capture your heart!

3⅓ c	**Filtered water (mixed use)**
1½ c	**Basmati brown rice, long grain, rinsed**
1 small	**Brown onion, sliced**
1	**Garlic clove, pressed**
1/2 tsp	**Tamari**
1/3 c	**Filtered water**

1) Bring 3 cups of water to a boil in a medium pan. Stir in the rice and cover. Reduce to simmer for 30 minutes, turn off heat and **do not** lift the lid for another 10 minutes.

2) Sauté onions and garlic in the remaining 1/3 cup of water and the tamari. Cover for a couple of minutes until water evaporates, then stir onions into rice.

3) Put everything into a food processor and blend. Using wet fingers (so mixture doesn't stick to your hands) pat into a pizza pan or into a pie dish*, forming a crust around perimeter. (Re-moisten fingers with water if rice gets too sticky.) Bake for 15 minutes in a preheated 450° oven.

Lightly sprayed with vegetable oil.

Garden Couscous

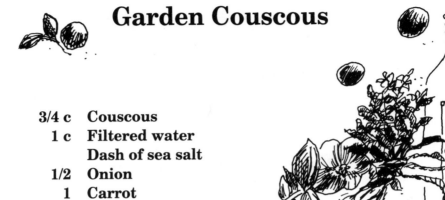

3/4 c	Couscous
1 c	Filtered water
	Dash of sea salt
1/2	Onion
1	Carrot
1/2 c	Peas
1	Garlic clove, pressed
1 Tbl	Liquid aminos
1/4 c	Fresh herbs, chopped (thyme, basil, mint, parsley, watercress, whatever you wish)
2 Tbl	Wine
	Cracked pepper

1) Heat the filtered water to a boil, add the couscous and sea salt. Return to a boil, cover for 5 minutes on low heat, then turn off.
2) Chop the veggies finely, put them into a skillet with the herbs, liquid aminos and wine. Sauté—add filtered water if necessary, cover and simmer until tender.
3) Fluff the couscous with a fork into the vegetable mix, stir to combine. Serve hot.

Serves 2-3

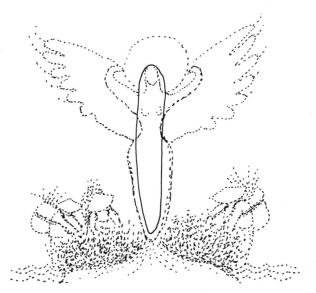

Natalia's Rice

A delicious Spanish-style rice.

3/4 c	**Basmati, jasmine or long grain rice**
1/2	**Lemon, juiced**
1/4 c	**White wine (or broth)**
1/4 c	**Salsa Fresca (page 144), or substitute 1 garlic clove, pressed; 1 tsp cumin; 1 Tbl onion, minced; 1 tomato, seeded and chopped**
1 c	**Hot filtered water**
1 Tbl	**Liquid aminos**

1) Rinse the rice and cover with the hot filtered water for 10 minutes, drain.
2) Pour the lemon juice over the rice, toss.
3) Heat the wine or broth in a skillet, add the rice, stir (about 5 minutes), add the salsa, the filtered water and seasoning, stir well. Cover and cook for 12-15 minutes.

Serves 2-3

Yellow Rice

The turmeric seasoning gives the rice a luscious yellow color,
and nicely complements green vegetables.

2 c	**Long grain brown rice**
4 c	**Boiling filtered water**
1½ tsp	**Turmeric**
2 tsp	**Sesame oil**
	Cracked pepper and 1 Tbl liquid aminos

1) Bring the filtered water to a boil, add the rinsed rice and seasonings.
2) Cover the pot and simmer for 30 minutes, then turn off the heat and keep the lid on for another 5-10 minutes. This method yields perfectly steam cooked rice.

Serves 4-6

Wild Rice

3 c	**Filtered water**
1 c	**Wild rice**
1/4 c	**Red wine**
1 small	**Red onion**
1/2 tsp	**Vegetable salt**

1) Bring the filtered water to a boil.
2) Dice the onion, rinse the rice.
3) Add all of the ingredients to the boiling water, cover and simmer for 1 hour.

Serves 2-3

Mustard Seed Quinoa

(pronounced keen-wa)

*Quinoa is an ancient supergrain and a complete protein,
containing the highest amount of essential fatty acids of any grain.
It has a light, nutty taste. The addition of mustard seeds and
Basmati rice give it an Indian flair.*

1 Tbl	Black mustard seeds
1 c	Quinoa, rinsed
1 c	Rice—jasmine or basmati (white), rinsed
3½ c	Filtered water
1/2 Tbl	Liquid aminos or 1/2 tsp sea salt
	Pinch of cayenne

1) Add the mustard seeds to a small hot skillet (have a lid ready
    to cover them once the seeds begin to pop). Turn off the heat
    after the seeds begin to pop.
2) Bring the filtered water to a boil, add the rinsed grains, and the
    remaining ingredients. Cover and cook on low for 15 minutes.

Serves 4-6

Toasted Anise Rice

1 c	Basmati rice
1/2 Tbl	Anise seeds
1¾ c	Filtered water
1/2 tsp	Sea salt

1) Bring the filtered water to a boil in a pot.
2) Toast the anise seeds in a toaster oven until they are light
    brown.
3) Add the seeds, rice and salt to the pot. Return to boil, then
    cover and simmer 15-20 minutes.

Serves 2-3

Quick Sushi Rice

For an authentic sushi rice flavor,
fold this sauce into cooked rice.

1½ Tbl	Rice vinegar
1 Tbl	Honey
1/2 Tbl	Soy sauce
	Dash of mirin
2 c	Cooked short grain brown rice

1) Heat up the sauce mixture in a small saucepan, stir to dissolve the mixture ingredients.
2) Cool the sauce mix to room temperature, then cut the sauce into rice with a large wooden paddle-spoon.

Miso Sesame Rice

1 c	Brown rice
2 c	Filtered water
1 Tbl	Tahini
1 Tbl	Miso
2 tsp	Onion powder
1/4 c	Warm filtered water

1) Bring the filtered water to a boil, add the rinsed rice, cover and simmer for 35-40 minutes. (Do not peek!)
2) Mix all of the remaining ingredients into a paste, then stir them into the rice when the rice is done.

Serves 2-3

Celebration Millet

Millet is celebrated in a unique way by pairing it with a green chutney. The mixture of fresh mint and cilantro, punctuated with citrus and garlic makes a terrific condiment by itself or to serve with Indian fare. Enjoy the aroma!

Green Chutney Sauce:

2	Jalapeños, seeded, chopped
1	Lemon, juiced
1	Orange, juiced
1/3 c	Coconut, flakes
1/2 c	Cilantro leaves, freshly chopped
1/2 c	Mint leaves, freshly chopped
1/3 c	Filtered water
1/4 tsp	Sea salt
1	Garlic clove, pressed

2½ c	Stock or filtered water
1 Tbl	Tamari
1¼ c	Millet, rinsed
2 Tbl	Pine nuts, lightly toasted
1 Tbl	Black mustard seeds
1/4 c	Raisins (golden ones)

1) Put the chutney ingredients into a food processor or a blender and blend well, stop and scrape down when necessary. Set aside.
2) Put the filtered water and tamari into a pot and bring them to a boil.
3) Stir in the millet and cover, simmer for 40-45 minutes.
4) Toss in the last three ingredients before serving, or use them as a garnish. Stir the chutney sauce into the millet or use it as a sauce or condiment.

*Serve with a crisp cucumber salad and **Tofu Marinade over Daikon** (page 269).*

Serves 2-4

Vegetable Polenta Frittata

2 Tbl	Liquid aminos
1	Onion, peeled and sliced
3/4 c	Eggplant, cubed
1/2 c	Mushrooms, quartered
1 lg	Garlic clove, pressed
2	Zucchinis, chopped
1/3 c	Instant cereal (brown rice cream, oat bran, cream of wheat)
	Broth or filtered water
2 Tbl each	Parsley, fresh, and low-fat soy parmesan cheese
1 tsp each	Oregano, basil and nutritional yeast
	Dash red chili flakes and curry

1) Heat the liquid aminos in a skillet, sauté the onions, the cubed and skinned eggplant, mushrooms, garlic, and zucchini.
2) Stir in the cereal, slowly add the broth or filtered water stirring to a smooth consistency. Add the herbs and spices and simmer for 3-5 minutes.
3) Pour into a non-stick ring mold, baking dish or pie dish and refrigerate until firm.
4) To serve: Slice the frittata and sauté it in a little liquid aminos (or heat it in the oven). Serve a sauce of your choice on the top. We like a simple marinara on the side.

If you like this recipe, try changing the spices and vegetables for a different flavor.

For Mexican, try green chiles and tomatoes sauteed with cumin and chili powder, serve with **Meximato Sauce** *(page 142).*

Serves 4

Mushroom Kasha

A savory mushroom and toasted buckwheat pilaf.

1 c	**Kasha**
1½ c	**Boiling filtered water (mixed use)**
1/2 lb	**Mushrooms (2 cups)**
1 sm	**Onion, peeled**
1 Tbl	**Liquid aminos**
1/4 c	**Red wine**
1	**Garlic clove**
1/2	**Lemon, juiced**
1/4 c	**Parsley, chopped**

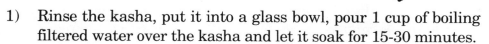

1) Rinse the kasha, put it into a glass bowl, pour 1 cup of boiling filtered water over the kasha and let it soak for 15-30 minutes.
2) Slice the mushrooms and onion, then sauté them in a large skillet with the liquid aminos, wine, garlic and lemon juice. Stir continuously for a couple of minutes.
3) Add the strained kasha and stir, add parsley.
4) Then add the rest of the filtered water, cover for 15 minutes on low heat. Fluff with a fork before serving.

Serves 4

Spiced Indian Dal

*Dal is a staple food in Indian cooking, it resembles small green split peas. Serve with a **Vegetable Curry***, **Mustard Seed (Quinoa) Rice*** and **Fig Chutney***.*

1/2 c	**Dal**
3¾ c	**Filtered water**
1 Tbl	**Onion seeds**
2 Tbl	**Liquid aminos**
1 tsp	**Chopped fresh skinned ginger**
1 lg	**Garlic clove, pressed**
1 tsp	**Coriander**
1/4 tsp	**Cardamom**
1 recipe for	**Mustard Seed Rice (page 205)**

1) Wash the dal (looks like small split peas).
2) Bring the filtered water to a boil in a medium pot.
3) Add the dal and onion seeds. Bring to a boil, cover and reduce to simmer for 30 minutes.
4) Press the ginger and garlic through a garlic press, and add to the pot along with the rest of the seasonings.
5) Puree dal in a blender for a smooth sauce, then transfer the dal back into the saucepan. Heat before serving over rice.

*See recipes on pages 264, 205, 153, respectively.

Serves 4

Outrageous Pot o'Beans

The aroma of homemade spicy beans can tantalize anyone!
This makes a large pot, and leftovers can be frozen.
Great in soups, with tortillas, or pureed into a sauce.

2 c	Your favorite dried beans (garbanzo, white, black, red, pinto)
2	Red California Chiles, dried (5" long)
1	Bell pepper, chopped
1	Onion, peeled and chopped
1½ c	Tomato puree (or crushed tomatoes)
5	Garlic cloves, minced
1 Tbl	Cumin seeds
2 Tbl	Onion powder
1 tsp each	Cumin powder, sweet basil, oregano, chile powder
	Dash of clove powder

1) Rinse the beans and put them into a large pot, cover with filtered water and let them soak overnight (10 hours).
2) Bring the filtered water in the pot to a boil, cover and simmer for 2 hours.
3) Add the chiles (break off their stem and shake out their seeds first). Cook another 20 minutes.
4) Add the rest of the ingredients, return to a boil on high, then simmer 1 more hour until soft.
5) Scrape the chile pulp from the skin and put the pulp back into the pot, throw away the skins—adjust the seasonings to your taste or add filtered water if needed.

Serves 6

Aduki Bean and Brown Rice Pot

Easy! Cook it all in one pot for a satisfying meal.

6 c	**Filtered water**
1 c	**Aduki beans, rinsed**
1 c	**Long grain brown rice, rinsed**
1	**Red onion, peeled and chopped**
1	**Bell pepper, seeded and chopped**
3	**Garlic cloves, minced**
1/4 tsp	**Cayenne**
2 tsp	**Cumin**
1 Tbl	**Chile powder**
1 tsp	**Vegetable salt**

1) Bring the filtered water to a boil, add the beans, and then return the pot to a boil. Cover and cook on low for 20 minutes.
2) Add the rice, chopped veggies and seasonings. Cover and simmer for 45 minutes to 1 hour.

*Serve with tortillas and a garnish of **Salsa Fresca** (quick recipe below, or see page 144):*

1/4 c	**Cilantro, chopped**
1 c	**Tomatoes, chopped**
1/2 c	**Onion, peeled and chopped**
1	**Jalapeño chile, seeded and chopped**
	Avocado slices on the side if desired)

Mix in one bowl.

Serves 6

Féjoada

(Fay-jo-wah´-dah)

*We substitute soy sausages in this
Brazilian staple of black beans
and vegetables.*

Beans:

2 qts	**Filtered water**
2 c	**Black beans**
1 tsp	**Ginger, skinned and pressed**

2 Tbl each	**Wine, lemon juice**
1/2 lb	**Soy sausage (spiced)**
1 Tbl	**Garlic, minced**
3/4 c	**Onions, peeled and sliced**
2	**Tomatoes, chopped**
1	**Jalapeño, roasted (see page 27)**
1/2 tsp	**Sea salt**
1/4 tsp	**Fresh ground black pepper**
2 tsp	**Grated orange rind**
	Cayenne to taste

1) Bring the filtered water to a boil, add the rinsed beans and ginger and boil for 2 minutes. Then cover and let the beans soak 1 hour (or soak overnight).

2) Return the pot to a boil, then turn to low. Simmer beans for 2 hours covered, until tender. Chop the vegetables.

3) Sauté the garlic and onion in the liquids in a big skillet. Add the soy sausages and cook for 5 minutes, add the rest of the ingredients.

4) Add the beans with a slotted spoon into the skillet, adding the bean liquid to thin. Simmer for 15 minutes or until thick. Turn the mixture often using a spatula. Féjoada can be frozen for future use.

Serve with tortillas or rice, salad, and a big platter of fruit with lime wedges for dessert.

Serves 6-8

🫘 Green Chile Corn Bread 🫘

A Southwest corn bread that is addicting.

1½ tsp	Egg replacer with 2 Tbl filtered water
1 c	"Lite" soy milk
2 Tbl	Oil (Canola or Safflower)
1 c	Wholewheat pastry or unbleached flour
1 c	Whole grain corn meal
3 Tbl	Date, turbinado or brown sugar
5 tsp	Baking powder
1 sm can	Green chiles, chopped
1/2 tsp each	Sea salt, cumin and onion powder
1 ear	Corn shredded (about 1/2 cup)

1) Stir the wet ingredients together (first 3 items).
2) Sift the dry ingredients into the wet. Stir in the chiles, corn and spices.
3) Place in a 9" non-stick baking pan and bake at 375° for 35 minutes or until light brown.

*Serve with **3 Pepper Black Bean Salad** (page 81).*

Tempeh Herb Bread

*A spicy round wheat bread with crumbled tempeh and the aroma
of Italian sausage.*

1/4 c	**Warm filtered water**
1 pk	**Active dry yeast**
3/4 c	**Warm "Lite" soy milk**
1 Tbl	**Honey**
2½ c	**Wholewheat pastry flour**
1/2 c	**Unbleached flour**
6 oz	**Tempeh cutlet***
1 Tbl	**Olive oil**
1 tsp each	**Soy sauce, basil, oregano, fennel seeds, red chile flakes, onion and garlic powder**

1) Sprinkle the yeast over the warm filtered water—let it sit for 5 minutes.

2) Heat the soy sauce and 1/2 of the oil, sauté crumbled tempeh on low, stirring for several minutes—set aside and stir in the herbs.

3) Add the soy milk and honey to the yeast, add flour 1 cup at a time. Knead it until smooth for about 6-10 minutes. Cover the dough and let it rise for an hour in a lightly oiled bowl.

4) Punch down the dough, spread it flat, work in the tempeh and form dough into a ball. Press an inverted can on top for an interesting shape. Let the dough rise for 30 minutes on a baking sheet.

5) Brush the dough with olive oil and bake at 375° for 30 minutes (should sound hollow if tapped), slice in wedges.

Makes 1 loaf

*Available in natural food stores.

VEGETABLE SIDE DISHES

♥ Fat Free

Baking Vegetables Whole

Vegetables with skins on them bake the best. Wash veggies first, and pierce potatoes with a fork to allow steam to escape (it's not necessary to pierce yams or sweet potatoes). Unpeeled beets, garlic and onions can be baked whole. Slice the bottoms off of onions and sit them in a shallow baking pan of filtered water so the dripping juices don't burn. Average temperature is 375° for baking.

Broiled Vegetables

For a change of pace try this quick method of using a hot 550° oven, use the top rack in your oven.

Your choice of vegetables: zucchini, eggplant, mushrooms, peppers, onions, fennel root

1) Slice the veggies thin to ensure even cooking.
2) Brush soft veggies with tamari, liquid aminos, or a garlic-herb-oil mixture so they don't dry out too fast.
3) Put the veggies on a cookie sheet, check them every couple of minutes because they cook fast! If the veggies brown quicker than they cook, move rack down one notch.

Try mushrooms (cap side down) with a drop of liquid aminos inside caps, skewer veggies and place them over a pan to catch their juice; or try eggplant slices topped with tomato sauce, herbs and soy cheese.

Steamed Vegetables with Dill

Fresh dill weed and chives dress up quickly steamed veggies
for a great side dish.

1 lg	Broccoli stalk
1/2 head	Cauliflower
2	Red rose potatoes (about 1½ cups)
2 Tbl	Dill, fresh, minced
1 Tbl	Chives, fresh, minced
1 Tbl	Lemon juice
1 Tbl	Liquid aminos
2 Tbl	Filtered water from steaming

1) Cut the broccoli into spears, skin and quarter the stalk. Break the cauliflower into florettes and cube the potatoes.
2) Put the steamer basket into a large pot, add filtered water to 1" deep, add the veggies and cover. Bring to a boil, then simmer until al dente (not too soft) about 10-12 minutes.
3) Remove the steamer basket full of veggies and set it aside. Transfer the steam water into another vessel.
4) Add the herbs and 2 Tbl of the stock (steam water) to the pot, add the veggies and toss them altogether with the rest of the ingredients.

*Serve warm with a grain dish like **Mushroom Kasha** (page 209).*

Serves 2-4

Ginger Longbeans

*Wonderful on **Cabbage Noodles** (page 268).*

1 bunch	Japanese long beans
12 med	Mushrooms
3	Celery ribs
1 Tbl	Ginger, skinned
1/4 c	Filtered water
1/4 c	Cooking sherry
1 Tbl	Tamari
1/2 tsp	Toasted sesame oil

1) Chop the beans in 2" lengths, slice the vegetables, and mince the ginger.
2) Heat the water in a wok on high, add the vegetables, cook for 8 minutes.
3) Stir in the last three items, turn off the heat and cover for a couple of minutes to warm.

Serves 4

Simmering Lotus Root

A slightly sweet and crisp side dish.

1 sm	Lotus root—2" diameter*
1½ c	Filtered water with some rice vinegar added

Sauce:

3 Tbl	Mirin
1 Tbl	Tamari
2 Tbl	Hot filtered water
pinch	Umeboshi paste
1 Tbl	Brown sesame seeds as garnish
	Dash of toasted sesame oil

1) Peel fresh lotus root, slice off their ends, then slice them thinly.
2) Put the lotus root into a saucepan with filtered water and vinegar. Bring it to a boil, then simmer on low for 10-15 minutes, drain off the water.
3) Stir the sauce ingredients together. Pour the sauce over the cooked roots in the same small pan, cooking briefly. Sprinkle the sesame seeds generously on top. (Top brown briefly for extra flavor).

Peeled, sliced and boiled lotus roots are found in oriental groceries. Omit steps 1 and 2 if whole lotus roots are not used.

Serves 4

Sauteed Fennel Bulk

An aromatic delicacy.

3-4	Whole fennel bulbs, sliced into "patties"
8 lg	Garlic cloves, unpeeled
2 Tbl	Olive oil
1/4 c	Filtered water
2 Tbl	Fennel leaves, chopped, as garnish
	Sea salt or liquid aminos and pepper to taste

1) Put 1 Tbl of filtered water into a skillet and bring it to medium high heat. Add the olive oil, then put in the fennel slices face down. Add garlics with jackets on (so they don't burn).
2) Stir, shake, and flip the fennel over when browned on each side.
3) Sprinkle with sea salt and pepper, pour filtered water in and cover for 20 minutes until tender.
4) Garnish with the fennel leaves.

Serves 4

New Zealand Spinach

New Zealand spinach is a type of spinach that has more texture and a shorter thicker leaf than regular spinach. If it is not available, try any other greens such as collards, escarole or chard.

1 Tbl	Filtered water
2 tsp	Safflower or olive oil
1	Garlic clove, minced
1 lg bunch	New Zealand spinach
	Sesame seeds, toasted as garnish

1) Heat the filtered water and oil in a wok, add garlic—stir.
2) Then add the cleaned greens—cover with 1/4 cup of filtered water. Steam for 5 minutes. Add a bit of soy sauce as a seasoning if desired.

Serves 2-3

Turnip Gratin

Try with other roots, too!

6	Turnips
1 Tbl	Liquid aminos
3/4	Tofu Cream Sauce (page 134)
1/4 c	Bread crumbs

1) Grate the turnips, then sauté them in a skillet in the liquid bouillon.
2) Put the turnips into a baking dish, cover them with the cream sauce.
3) Top with 1/4 cup of the bread crumbs and bake 30 minutes at 375°.

Serves 6

Chayote Squash and Corn

A Native American dish.

2	Chayotes, cut into chunks
2 ears	Corn, shucked and cut off the cob
1	Garlic clove, pressed
2 Tbl	Red peppers or pimentos, roasted and chopped
3 Tbl	Filtered water
1 Tbl	Liquid aminos

1) Cut the squash into chunks and remove the core—then steam for 10 minutes. Remove the skin. Put the chayote into a pot with the remaining ingredients.
2) Bring to a boil with the lid on, then simmer on low for 20 or so minutes until tender.

*Serve with **Garden Couscous** (page 202) or toss into a pasta.*

Serves 4

Spaghetti Squash Americana

Makes 4 moderate servings—but it is so delicious, you may wish to double the recipe and freeze leftovers. Kids go for this, too.

1/2	**Spaghetti squash**
1/2 c	**Soy cheese, grated**
1 clove	**Garlic, pressed**
	Fresh cracked black pepper
	Nutmeg—freshly grated is best

1) Scoop the seeds out of the squash and steam in a large pot with a bit of water for 45 minutes, until the squash is tender.
2) Scoop the flesh out of the squash and stir it in a bowl with the rest of the goodies, season to taste.

Serve steamed vegetables on top with fresh grated soy cheese and lemon juice. Zucchinis, mushrooms and bell peppers are nice.

Serves 2-4

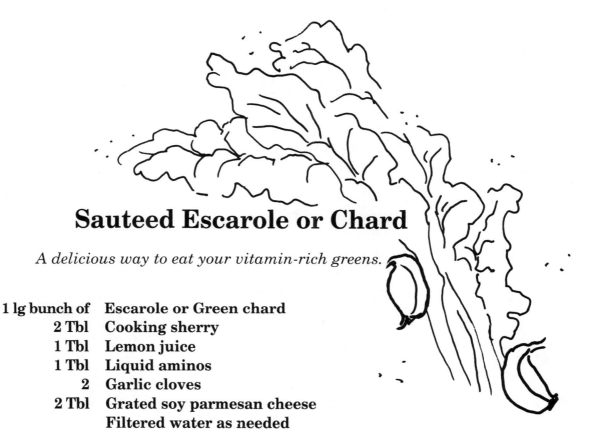

Sauteed Escarole or Chard

A delicious way to eat your vitamin-rich greens.

1 lg bunch of	**Escarole or Green chard**
2 Tbl	**Cooking sherry**
1 Tbl	**Lemon juice**
1 Tbl	**Liquid aminos**
2	**Garlic cloves**
2 Tbl	**Grated soy parmesan cheese**
	Filtered water as needed

1) Slice the greens. If using chard, cut out the ribs in a "V" shape, slice the ribs.
2) Sauté the greens in the liquids in a heavy skillet. Stir frequently on low heat for 10 minutes.
3) Press the garlic on top of the sauté when the greens are almost done, toss in the soy parmesan. Drizzle a bit of olive oil on top if desired. Serve warm.

Serve with **Celebration Millet** *(page 207) or a slice of* **Vegetable Polenta Frittata** *(page 208).*

Serves 2-4

Swedish Red Cabbage

Serves 4 as a side dish—great with hearty foods like broiled tempeh and potatoes, yields a sweet-sour taste—good chilled too.

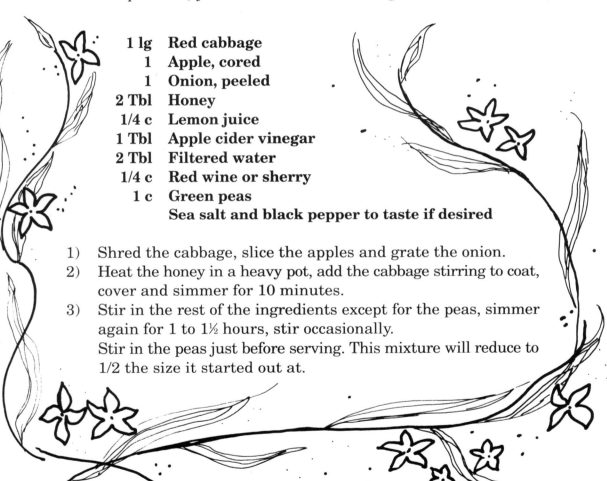

1 lg	Red cabbage
1	Apple, cored
1	Onion, peeled
2 Tbl	Honey
1/4 c	Lemon juice
1 Tbl	Apple cider vinegar
2 Tbl	Filtered water
1/4 c	Red wine or sherry
1 c	Green peas
	Sea salt and black pepper to taste if desired

1) Shred the cabbage, slice the apples and grate the onion.
2) Heat the honey in a heavy pot, add the cabbage stirring to coat, cover and simmer for 10 minutes.
3) Stir in the rest of the ingredients except for the peas, simmer again for 1 to 1½ hours, stir occasionally.
   Stir in the peas just before serving. This mixture will reduce to 1/2 the size it started out at.

Sherried Shrooms

A magical side dish for two.

10 lg	Mushrooms, quartered
1/2 c	Cooking sherry
4	Garlic cloves, pressed
1 tsp each	Onion powder and soy sauce
	Filtered water as needed

1) Heat the sherry in a skillet, add the garlic, stir, then add the mushrooms and continue stirring on medium heat.
2) Add the rest of the ingredients and simmer for about 10 more minutes.

Jamaican Eggplant

Succulent eggplants in a coconut spiced sauce.

2 sm	Eggplants
1	Red bell pepper, sliced
1 lg	Garlic clove, pressed
1"	Piece ginger, skinned and pressed
1/4 c	Coconut milk
1/4 c	Filtered water
1/2	Lemon, juiced
	Sea salt, black pepper and cayenne to taste

1) Skin and halve the eggplants, slice into 1/4" thick semi-circles.
2) Heat the lemon juice, filtered water and coconut milk in a wok.
3) Sauté the vegetables in a hot wok until tender, for about 5-10 minutes.

Serves 3-4

Whipped Eggplant

*You can serve this warm as a side dish or
chilled as a dip for pita bread.*

2 sm	**Eggplants**
1	**Lemon, juiced**
2	**Garlic, cloves**
1/2 tsp	**Curry powder**
2 Tbl	**Tahini**
2 tsp	**Tamari**
pinch	**Cayenne and cracked pepper**

1) Slice the eggplants lengthwise, lightly salt and leave them to sweat for 15 minutes.
2) Blot off the water and salt with a paper towel and bake the eggplants at 400° for 30 minutes.
3) When the eggplants are cool, remove their skin, chop their flesh and put the chopped eggplant into a blender or a food processor with all of the remaining ingredients. Puree until smooth.

Or serve as a soup—thin to consistency desired.

Serves 4-6

Potatoes, Peppers & Ale

A spicy and hearty side dish. The Ale will carmelize in heat and create a fantastic seasoning.

3 lg	**Russet potatoes**
1 lg	**Onion, peeled**
1	**Anaheim pepper**
2	**Jalapeño peppers**
1/4 c	**Dark beer or ale**
1 Tbl	**Tamari or Bronner's**
	Cracked pepper
1/2 c	**Grated soy cheese, cheddar style**

1) Peel and cube the potatoes in 1/2" sections.
2) De-seed the peppers and slice them along with the onion.
3) Put the potatoes and onions in a baking dish and toss them with the rest of the ingredients (except for the soy cheese). Bake at 400° for 45 minutes. Stir in the soy cheese when done.

Serves 4

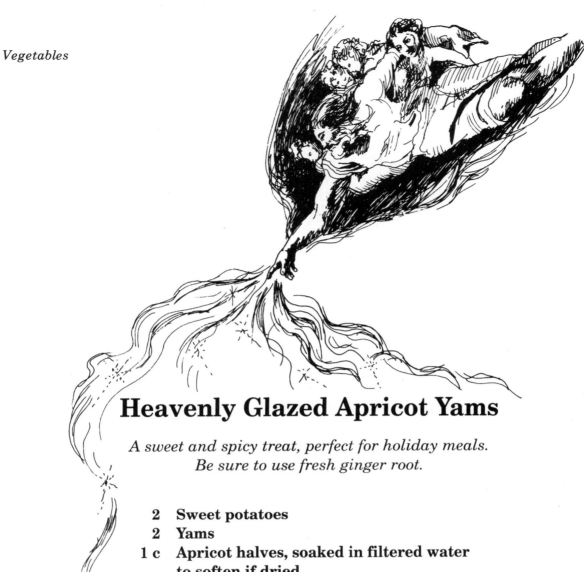

Heavenly Glazed Apricot Yams

A sweet and spicy treat, perfect for holiday meals.
Be sure to use fresh ginger root.

2	**Sweet potatoes**
2	**Yams**
1 c	**Apricot halves, soaked in filtered water** **to soften if dried**
1/4 c	**Lemon juice**
1/4 c	**Maple syrup or honey**
1 Tbl	**Ginger, skinned and freshly chopped**
	Fresh grated nutmeg

1) Bake the yams and the potatoes until tender, about 35 minutes at 350°.
2) Meanwhile, stir the lemon juice, maple syrup and ginger together (press the ginger through a garlic press to release its flavor).
3) Peel and slice the tubers, arrange half of the tubers on a glass baking dish. Pour half of the lemon mix on top of them, then arrange half of the apricots on top, repeat the process with the second layer.
4) Bake until warmed in a 375° oven (about 15-20 minutes).

6-10 servings

MAIN DISHES

Please note: Wonderful main dishes can be made from the recipes in the *Grains and Beans* chapter: (e.g., *Vegetable Frittata*, and *Aduki Bean and Brown Rice Pot*). Try combining some of the recipes from this chapter along with the recipes from the *Vegetable Side Dishes* chapter for a real treat.

♥ Fat Free

MAIN DISHES

At last, an eclectic montage of vegetarian main dishes prepared without dairy products. These dishes provide a down home comfort, and yet aspire to new and unusual global gastronomical sensations.

Our fascination with other cultures and foods has led to many adventurous experiments as you will see in the following recipes.

These multi-ethnic dishes include American nouvelle cooking, exotic south of the border creations, crowd pleasing Italian entrees, Thai delights, and other vegetarian favorites; all prepared with your ultimate health in mind.

These dishes will leave you feeling lighter than the foods you might be used to eating. We have many titillating tofu and tempeh recipes that will expand your knowledge and use of them, while stretching your food budget.

Using your imagination to combine these new foods will lead you to exciting and innovative meals. May you too have the courage to create and expand your gustatory vocabulary.

Acorn Squash Flowers

*Sliced acorn squash is stuffed with toasted almond rice and served with a **Spinach Mint Sauce**. An Autumn delight!*

1	Acorn Squash
1 c	Brown rice, rinsed
1/4 c	Almonds, chopped
1/2 Tbl	Soy or tamari
1 lg	Garlic clove, pressed
1/2 c	Fresh chopped mint
	Cayenne
	Spinach Mint Sauce (page 133)

1) Slice the squash crossways in half, then remove the seeds. Steam the squash in a bit of filtered water in a large pot for 10-12 minutes. Check with a fork to test firmness (should be firm yet tender—mushy doesn't work). Remove the squash and let it cool, then slice it into 1" thick "flowers". Skin the squash flowers, being careful not to lose their petal shaped outside. Make sure the spines are removed in the valleys between the scalloped part of the squash flowers.

2) Cook the rice in 2 cups of filtered water for 30 minutes (Basmati rice is the most fragrant).

3) Toast the almonds until they are lightly brown. Stir the soy, garlic, mint and cayenne into the cooked rice.

4) Mound the rice inside the squash "flowers" and bake them in a preheated oven for 15 minutes at 300-350° until warm.

5) Spoon 1/4 cup of the sauce on the bottom of each plate. Place a stuffed squash ring on top, sprinkle with mint and serve the sauce on the side in a gravy server.

Serve with tomato wedges and a crusty bread if desired.

Serves 4

Barbequed Tempeh

For summer fun, try these as burgers.

1 (8 oz) pk	**Tempeh, halved**

BBQ Sauce:

1½ Tbl	**Natural ketchup**
1 Tbl each	**Honey and onion powder**
1 tsp each	**Tamari and lemon juice**
1/4 tsp	**Cayenne**
1	**Garlic clove, pressed**
	Few drops toasted sesame oil
	(brushed on last after cooking)

1) Steam the tempeh for 10 minutes.
2) Mix the sauce ingredients together.
3) Brush the sauce over both sides of the tempeh filets and barbeque or broil them for 10 minutes on each side.

Serve with corn on the cob and salad, or make into tempeh barbeque burgers—add buns and trimmings.

Serves 2

∿ Savory Stuffed Zucchini ∿

Enjoy your foot long zucchinis with this exotic stuffing.
*Serve with **Satin Sauce** drizzled on top.*

1 lg	Zucchini (about 1'x4" thick)
2 Tbl each	White wine, lemon juice *and* liquid aminos
1¼ c	Celery, finely chopped
1¼ c	Onion, peeled and chopped
3/4 c	Yellow wax peppers (seed if you don't like "hot")
1¼ c	Tomatoes, seeded and chopped
2	Garlic cloves, pressed
1/2 c	Sunflower seeds, lightly toasted
1/4 c	Currants
1/2 tsp each	Cumin seeds, freshly grated orange peel
1 tsp each	Cumin and coriander powder
1 c	Crumbled firm tofu
	Pinch of sage and sea salt
1 recipe	Satin Sauce (page 139)

1) Trim the ends off the zucchini, halve it lengthwise and scoop out the inner flesh leaving a 1/2" thick shell. Sprinkle the zucchini insides with the liquid aminos. Chop the zucchini flesh and set it aside for the stuffing. Pre-bake the zucchinis at 375° for 25 minutes.

2) Meanwhile make the stuffing: heat the liquids in a deep large skillet on medium heat, adding the veggies and spices in the order given. Stir in 2 cups of chopped zucchini flesh, simmer for 10-15 minutes.

3) Stuff the zucchini shell. Line a cookie sheet with foil, place the stuffed zucchini shell on top (pour 1/4 cup of filtered water on a cookie sheet), and bake at 375° for 45 minutes.

4) To serve, pour the warmed Satin Sauce on top of the stuffed zucchini.

Serves 4

Spinach Tofu Loaf

*A healthy meat-less loaf accented with toasted seeds and topped with the **Soygurt Dill Sauce** below.*

1 lb	"Lite" tofu
1 pk	Frozen spinach, chopped
1/4 c	Toasted seeds (sunflower, pinenuts or walnuts)
1/4 c	Fine bread crumbs
1 Tbl each	Dill and onion powder
2 tsp	Herbamare or vegetable salt
1/2	Lemon, juiced
2	Garlic cloves, pressed
	Dash of Cayenne
1/2 tsp	Lemon pepper

Stir all of the ingredients together and place them in a non-stick casserole dish. Sprinkle bread crumbs on top, bake at 375° for 20 minutes.

Soygurt Dill Sauce

1/2 c	Soy yogurt, plain
2 Tbl	Tofu Mayo (page 150)
1 tsp each	Dill and lemon juice

Whip together and serve on the side.

Serves 4-6

Mushroom Seitan in Wine Sauce with Wild Rice

A seductive dish for those desiring a "meaty" taste.

12 oz	Spicy seitan, slice in 1/4" thick cutlets
1/4 c	Red wine
1/2	Lemon, juiced
1	Garlic clove, minced
2 c	Mushrooms, sliced

Gravy:

1/2 tsp	Arrowroot powder—mixed with the juice from the seitan package, stir well

Wild Rice (page 204)
Parsley as garnish

1) Heat the wine, lemon, garlic and mushrooms in a skillet. Sauté until the mushrooms are tender. Add the gravy, heat and stir until the sauce thickens.
2) Add the seitan and heat until warm.
3) Make a bed of rice on each plate, lay the seitan slices on top of each bed of rice, pour the gravy on top.

Serve with a crisp salad or steamed vegetables.

Serves 2-3

Mushroom Tofu Loaf

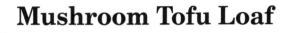

1 c	Mushrooms
1 c	Onions, peeled
1/2 c	Celery
1 Tbl	Liquid aminos
1 Tbl	Cooking sherry
1	Garlic clove, pressed
2 c	"Lite" silken tofu
1/2 c	Fine bread crumbs
1 c	Jalapeño soy cheese, grated
1 Tbl	Egg replacer mixed with 4 Tbl filtered water
1 Tbl	Lemon juice
	Pinch of cayenne, dill, Italian seasoning
1 tsp	Coriander powder

1) Slice the mushrooms, chop the onions, mince the celery.
2) Sauté the veggies in the liquid aminos and sherry until they are tender.
3) Put the sauteed vegetables into a medium bowl and add the rest of the ingredients, stir well. Transfer the loaf into a non-stick baking dish or loaf pan.
4) Bake at 425° for 35 minutes.

*Serve warm with **Mushroom Gravy** (page 131) and a large salad, or chilled with tomato slices.*

Broiled Tofu with Mushrooms

A very tasty layered tofu "Lasagne".

1 lb	**Tofu, sliced into 4 sections**
1½ c	**Mushrooms, sliced**
1/2	**Bunch green onions, minced**

Sauce:

2	**Garlic cloves, pressed**
1/4 c	**Red wine**
1/4 c	**Liquid aminos**
	Cayenne to taste
1/2 Tbl	**Chile sesame oil or toasted sesame oil**

1) Stir the sauce ingredients together.
2) Layer the ingredients by alternately placing the tofu, sauce, mushrooms, sauce, etc. in a casserole dish.
3) Broil at 450° for 35-45 minutes. Sprinkle the green onions on top after 30 minutes.

*Serve with **Wild Rice** (page 204) and a crunchy romaine salad.*

Serves 2-3

Roasted Tempeh with Pineapple Salsa

An Indonesian delight, served skewered or baked in a casserole.

8 oz pk	**Tempeh**
2 Tbl each	**Lemon juice and white wine**
1	**Garlic clove, pressed**
1 tsp	**Ginger, skinned and pressed**
1/4 c	**Liquid aminos**
1	**Bell pepper, sliced**
1	**Onion, peeled and sliced**
	Pineapple Salsa (page 144)

1) Cut the tempeh in half, then crossways to create 4 filets—steam the tempeh for 10 minutes.
2) Mix the next 4 ingredients together, pour the mixture over the tempeh and marinate the filets for 3 hours or more.
3) Put the tempeh filets on a non-stick baking dish, and place slivered onions and peppers around them—or skewer them shishkabob style.
4) Bake for 25 minutes at 400° until kabobs are tender. (Or cook the kabobs on the grill or barbeque.)

*Serve with **Pineapple Salsa** for a real taste sensation.*

Serves 2-3

Tofu Stuffed Tomatoes

A light, low calorie meal.

4	**Tomatoes**
1½ c	**Tofu*, mashed (firm is best)**
1/2 c	**Minced celery**
1/3 c	**Onion, peeled and minced**
1 Tbl	**Liquid aminos**
1/4 c	**Black olives**
1½ Tbl	**Lemon juice**
1/2 tsp each	**Dill weed and onion powder**
	Cayenne and gomasio to taste
1 Tbl	**Nutritional yeast**

1) Slice the tops off of the tomatoes, hollow the tomatoes out. Reserve 1/2 cup of the tomato flesh (seeds removed) for filling.
2) Sauté the onions and celery in the liquid aminos until tender.
3) Lightly stir all of the ingredients (including the tomato flesh) together, fill the tomato shells with the stuffing.
4) Garnish with sesame seeds or cilantro and serve raw.

Serve with assorted vegetables and sprouts, whole grain toast and parsley garnish.

*Try "lite" firm tofu by Mori Nu

Serves 4

Tempeh Cabbage Rolls

These cabbage rolls look festive from using both red and green cabbage leaves. Serve with steamed whole baby potatoes and broccoli.

Filling:

2 Tbl each	Cooking sherry and red wine
1/2	Lemon, juiced
1	Onion, peeled and minced
1	Carrot, minced
9 oz	Tempeh cutlet, steamed 5 minutes
	To taste: sea salt, black pepper, dill and cumin
	Toasted sesame oil
1 sm	Red cabbage
1 sm	Green cabbage

Sauce:

28 oz	Crushed Italian tomatoes
1 tsp	Dill weed
1/4 tsp	Cayenne
2	Garlic cloves, pressed
	Filtered water as needed

1) To make the filling: Heat the sherry, wine and lemon juice in a heavy skillet. Add the onion and the carrot, cook on medium heat until soft.

2) Crumble the tempeh into the skillet, stir and season to taste—set aside.

3) Steam the cabbages whole in a big pot, for 10-15 min. until their leaves are soft. Separate the cabbage leaves and cut thick rib pieces out of each cabbage.

4) Lay a cabbage leaf flat, put a spoonful of the filling in its center and roll it up burrito-style. Place the cabbage rolls in a baking dish, alternating the cabbage colors.

5) Stir the sauce ingredients together. Heat gently, then pour the sauce over the cabbage rolls. Cover and bake at 375° for 40-45 minutes.

Serves 4-6

Bon Temp Tofu Creole

"A whole lotta flavor going on", capturing the spirit of New Orleans in this savory stew.

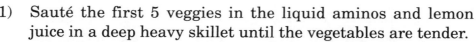

1	Onion, peeled and minced
1	Carrot, minced
2	Celery ribs, sliced
2	Garlic cloves, minced
2 lg	Bell peppers, chopped into 1" strips
2 Tbl	Liquid aminos
2 Tbl	Lemon juice
1 Tbl	Cajon Spice (page 154)
1 lb	Firm tofu cubed ("Lite")
1/2 c	Green peas
2	Tomatoes, seeded, chopped
1 c	Tomato sauce
6 oz	Tomato paste
2 c	Filtered water
2 Tbl	Cooking sherry or beer

1) Sauté the first 5 veggies in the liquid aminos and lemon juice in a deep heavy skillet until the vegetables are tender.
2) Add the cajon spice, tofu and all of the remaining ingredients, stirring all the while.
3) Cook the creole covered for 1 hour on simmer.

Serve over rice or noodles, you can freeze the sauce for later use.

Serves 6

Blackened Tofu (or Tempeh)

Marinated tofu "breaded" with a spicy Cajun seasoning and broiled.
A succulent way to enjoy tofu, also good as a snack or picnic item.
Serve with vegetables.

Preheat oven to Broil 550°

1 lb	Firm "Lite" tofu (press between towels to rid tofu of excess water)
1 Tbl	Lemon juice (mixed with liquid aminos)
1 Tbl	Liquid aminos
1½ Tbl	Cajun spice blend (page 154)

1) Slice the tofu into 1/2" thick filets, then cut each filet crosswise and lengthwise yielding 2"x2" cutlets. Marinate the cutlets in the juices for a minimum of 30 minutes.

2) Put the spice blend into a plastic bag, add the tofu cutlets and gently shake the cutlets to coat them evenly.

3) Lay the tofu cutlets onto a broiling pan (ventilated so they will get crisp) on the top rack of the oven. Broil the top side for 7-9 minutes, turn and broil the bottom side for 7-9 minutes—or barbeque!

Note: for Tempeh, steam the Tempeh for 15 minutes before marinating.

Serves 3-4

Tofu in a Jalapeño Vinaigrette

A hot vinegar marinade gives tofu a sizzle.

8 oz	"Lite" tofu, sliced into 2 thin squares
2 Tbl	Apple cider vinegar
1 Tbl	Cooking sherry
1 Tbl	Filtered water
1/2 tsp	Jalapeño, roasted and diced
	Pinch of sea salt and cracked black pepper
1	Cucumber, peeled and seeded

1) Sea salt and pepper the tofu cutlets. Sauté the tofu in the above mixture on medium high heat, cooking both sides.
2) Transfer the tofu to a shallow casserole dish.

Serve on a bed of "Cucumber Pasta"—Cut the cucumber into long fine strips. (1/16" wide x 6" long).

Serves 2

Tofu Enchiladas

A creamy tofu filling complements the tasty red chile sauce.

1 recipe	Chile Roja Enchilada sauce (page 129)

Filling:

1½ c	Crumbled "Lite" firm tofu
1 c	Grated soy jalapeño cheese
1/2	Bunch green onions, minced
2	Garlic cloves, pressed
1 c	Corn kernels
1 tsp each	Cumin and onion powder
	Fresh grated nutmeg and peppercorns
	Liquid aminos or a dash of sea salt

1 dozen	Corn tortillas

Topping:

	Sliced black olives
1/2 c	Grated soy cheese
	Thinly sliced onions
	Cilantro leaves

1) Prepare the enchilada sauce. Spread a little of the sauce on the bottom of a baking or casserole dish.
2) Mix together the tofu filling.
3) Heat the corn tortillas on a griddle until soft and warm.
4) Dip a hot tortilla into the sauce, then place a large spoonful of stuffing horizontally on the tortilla and roll it up.
5) Do this one tortilla at a time, placing each one on a baking dish as you go.
6) Cover with sauce, garnish with the last 4 items. Bake 1/2 hour at 350°.

Serves 6

Chile Verde Enchiladas

*These enchiladas are stuffed with sauteed squash and tofu cubes and baked in the luscious **Chile Verde Sauce**.*

1 recipe	Chile Verde Sauce (page 130)
1 c	Yellow squash (pumpkin or butternut)
1 lb	"Lite" firm tofu
1 c	Zucchini, sliced
1	Onion, peeled and sliced
2	Garlic cloves, pressed
1 Tbl	Lemon juice
1/4 tsp each	Nutmeg and black pepper
2 Tbl	Liquid aminos
1 tsp	Oregano
2 dz	Corn tortillas
1½ c	Shredded soy jalapeño cheese
	Cilantro as garnish

1) Prepare the Chile Verde Sauce, have it ready on the side.
2) Steam the squash until crisp-tender, not mushy.
3) Cut the tofu and squash into 1/2" cubes. Sauté them with the sliced zucchini, onions and garlic in lemon juice, liquid aminos and spices. Stir until coated.
4) Heat the tortillas on a griddle until soft, and fill with a heaping spoonful of the filling. Top with some soy cheese, then roll up the tortilla and place it on a non-stick baking dish. Cover with the Chile Verde Sauce.
5) Cover the enchiladas with foil and bake at 375° for 25 minutes. Uncover, then lay the rest of the soy cheese on top, and bake uncovered for 10 minutes.

These make good leftovers, they can also be frozen.

Serves 8-10

Tempeh Burritos

A very easy dish, make the filling ahead and reheat.

1/2	**Lemon, juiced**
1 tsp	**Liquid aminos**
1 Tbl	**Filtered water**
1 lg	**Garlic clove, pressed**
1	**Jalapeño, seeded and chopped**
6 oz	**Cubed tempeh (plain or marinated)**
30 oz	**Refried beans (vegetarian) or 3½ cups of your own**
1 tsp	**Cumin powder or crushed cumin seeds**
2	**Tomatoes, seeded and chopped**
1/2 Tbl	**Chile powder**
1 pk	**Soft tortillas of your choice**

1) Heat the liquids in a saucepan on med/high.
2) Add the garlic, jalapeño and tempeh, stir continuously for 5 minutes.
3) Add the rest of the seasonings and beans, stir well and then simmer.
4) Heat up the tortillas in an oven or on a griddle until soft and warm. Fill the tortillas up with the bean filling, then put the burritos in a baking dish or individual serving dishes. Keep them warm in the oven until ready to serve.

Burrito Options

Pour an enchilada sauce on top of the burritos, cover with grated soy cheese, olives, and green onions; bake for 20 minutes at 450°. Or, let everyone make and stuff their own tortillas by supplying dishes of:

- Shredded lettuce or cabbage
- Grated soy cheese
- Tomatoes
- Avocados or guacamole

Serves 5-6

Tomatillo Enchilada Casserole

A circular layered enchilada, slice like a pie.
You may also add sauteed zucchini or eggplant slices,
mushrooms or corn kernels to the filling.

1 dz	Corn tortillas
1 c	Cactus salsa (page 143) or Chile Verde Sauce* (page 130)
1 lb	"Lite" tofu
1 c	Jalapeño soy cheese, grated
2	Green onions, chopped
2	Garlic cloves, pressed
1/2	Lemon, juiced
	Vegetable salt, cumin to taste
	Soy Parmesan cheese

1) Pulse chop the tofu with the next 5 items in a food processor or a blender.
2) Heat the tortillas on a hot griddle until both sides are hot.
3) In a circular casserole baking dish, layer the salsa on the bottom, a tortilla, the filling, another swirl of salsa, a tortilla etc., until the baking dish is full. Top with the soy cheese.
4) Bake at 400° for 25 minutes.

*You may also use an 8 oz jar of green tomatillo salsa.

Serves 4

Tofu Mexicana

A layered Mexican casserole that serves two generously.

1 c	Enchilada sauce (page 129)
8 slices	"Lite" tofu, firm (approx. 10 oz.) 1/4" thickness
2	Tofu pups, sliced (Tofu hot dogs)
1	Green onion, sliced
1/4 c	Shredded soy cheddar cheese
1/2 c	Corn kernels cut off cob
	Garnish with fresh cilantro leaves

1) Pour a bit of enchilada sauce into a round baking dish.
2) Layer the tofu slices, pups, onions, soy cheese, corn, more sauce, tofu slices, etc. until the baking dish is full. Cover with foil and bake at 425° for 35 minutes or until bubbly.

Chile Rellenos

Hip hip hooray, an eggless dairyless relleno that is delicious!

6	Green Anaheim or California chiles
6	1/2" strips of soy cheese
1/4 c	Egg replacer mixed with
2/3 c	Filtered water
4 Tbl	Wholewheat pastry flour
1/8 tsp	Turmeric
1/4 tsp	Cumin

Serve with Meximato Sauce (page 142) or Enchilada sauce (page 129)

1) Wash and dry the chiles. Put them on a broiler rack and toast them in an oven at only 1" below broiler. Turn the chiles often so they don't get burned, only blistered and toasted.
2) Put the chiles into a plastic bag to cool, peel them carefully when they are cool.
3) Slice the chiles lengthwise, remove their pith and seeds and put 1 cheese strip inside (keep stems on the chiles for handling and visual presentation).
4) Whip the egg replacer with filtered water until thick, stir in the flour and spices. This is the batter.
5) Place a spoonful of the batter in a heated non-stick pan, lay a stuffed chile on top, cover with the batter and cook until one side is crisp, then turn the chile gently and cook the other side.
6) Keep the chiles warm on a plate in the oven, at 375°, until ready to serve.

*Pour **Meximato Sauce** (page 142) on top of the Chile Rellenos and garnish with cilantro. Serve with a side of black beans and a salad.*

Serves 2 generously

Polenta
with Fennel Tempeh Sauce

A hearty savory meal for hungry eaters.

Polenta:

3¼ c	Filtered water
1/2 tsp	Sea salt
1 c	Coarse grain corn meal (polenta)
1/3 c	Grated soy Parmesan

Sauce:

2	Fennel bulbs
6	Garlic cloves
1 Tbl	Cold pressed vegetable oil of choice
2 Tbl	Wine
8 oz	Tempeh
8 oz	Mushrooms
1 Tbl	Italian Herbs
2 lg	Tomatoes
6 oz can	Tomato sauce with filtered water to thin
1/2 tsp	Sage

1) Prepare the Polenta—bring the water to a boil, add salt and pour in the polenta in a thin stream stirring with a whisk constantly until it begins to thicken at a low heat. Keep stirring for 20 minutes until done, remove from the heat, stir in the soy cheese.

2) Coarsely chop the fennel, mince the garlic and sauté them in the wine and oil with the cubed tempeh for 5 minutes.

3) Add 1 cup of filtered water and cover on low heat for 15 minutes.

4) Add the quartered mushrooms, seeded chopped tomatoes and spices—turn into a sauce by stirring in the tomato paste and filtered water.

Serve sauce over polenta, garnish with fennel sprigs.

Serves 4

Pesto Mushroom Manicotti

*Mushrooms and pesto blend with soy cheese
for this epicurean medley.*

1 lb	**Parboiled shells or manicotti**
2 lbs	**Mushrooms, quartered**
1	**Onion, peeled and chopped**
8	**Garlic cloves, pressed**
1½ Tbl	**Liquid aminos**
2 tsp	**Olive oil**
1/4 c	**Red wine**
4 c	**Loose pack basil leaves**
	Fresh grated nutmeg and black pepper
4 Tbl	**Seasoned bread crumbs**
1 c	**Soy cheese, grated**

1) Sauté the mushrooms, onion and garlic in liquid aminos, red wine and oil until tender.
2) Transfer the vegetables to a food processor and pulse chop them until they are pureed, add the basil and the rest of the ingredients. Chop until just mixed.
3) Stuff the shells and arrange them on a baking dish with a bit of sauce* on the bottom. Put the sauce on top, cover with foil and bake for 30 minutes at 375°.

Serve with **Pinenut Bechamel Sauce (page 135) or **Tomato Vegetable Cream Sauce** (page 131) or just your favorite marinara.*

Serves 4-6

Tempeh Eggplant Parmesan

A high protein dish without a lot of soy cheese, easy to prepare and good for you.

1	Eggplant, sliced into rounds
1 (8 oz) pk	Tempeh halved, and cut lengthwise
4	Mushrooms, sliced
1/4 c	Fresh oregano, chopped
	Grated soy Parmesan
2 c	Your favorite Italian red sauce (with extra garlic)

1) Steam the tempeh and eggplant (if you wish, you can sauté the eggplant in 1 Tbl of wine and garlic). Preheat the oven to 400°.

2) Put 2 Tbl red sauce in a baking dish and layer 1/2 of the ingredients in the following order: eggplant, oregano, soy Parmesan, tempeh, mushrooms, sauce, then repeat until all of the ingredients are used. Reserve enough of the red sauce for the top, which is then followed by another grating of soy Parmesan and a pretty garnish of 3 mushroom slices. Make it your masterpiece!

3) Bake for 25 minutes at 400° or so, until heated throughout.

Serve with a large salad (spinach is nice), or on a platter of polenta.

Serves 4

Pesto Pasta

Fragrant basil makes a delicious sauce for fresh pasta.

1 lb	Pasta, fresh is best
1 Recipe	Pesto Sauce (page 149)
2-3 Tbl	Filtered hot water (from pasta)
2 Tbl	Toasted pine nuts
	Extra soy Parmesan for top

1) Cook pasta al dente, drain.
2) Spoon the water into the pesto to thin it and then stir the pesto into the pasta.
3) Garnish with nuts and soy Parmesan cheese.

Serves 4 generously

Marinara Love Sauce over Spaghetti Squash

A favorite vegetable sauce, served over steaming squash "pasta" served in its own shell.

Sauce:

1	Onion
4 Tbl	Red wine (chianti)
1 tsp	Olive oil
2	Garlic cloves
1	Bell pepper, diced
1 c	Mushrooms, sliced
28 oz	Crushed tomatoes
1/4 tsp each	Crushed red chile flakes and cracked black pepper
1/2 tsp each	Crushed fennel seeds and Basil (or use a fresh sprig)
2 Tbl	Soy Parmesan, grated

1) Heat 2 Tbl of the wine and the oil in a large skillet on a medium high heat. Add the onions, garlic and peppers—stirring gently until tender.
2) Stir in the tomatoes, mushrooms, herbs and wine, let it simmer.
3) After 1/2 hr., stir in the soy cheese, salt, pepper, and filtered water to thin it if necessary. Meanwhile, prepare the squash recipe on the next page.

Serves 2-4

Squash "pasta"

      1 lg   **Spaghetti squash**
      1 Tbl   **Grated soy Parmesan cheese**
               Fresh grated nutmeg and black pepper to taste

1) Prick the squash with a fork and bake for 30 minutes (or until shell is tender) in a 350° oven.
2) Split the shell in half when cool. Scoop out the seeds, discard them, then scoop out the flesh into a bowl (reserve the squash shells).
3) Mix the squash flesh with the rest of the ingredients. Keep the squash mixture warm in an oven.
4) Spoon 1/2 of the squash mixture into each 1/2 of the shell, spoon the sauce on top. Serve. Garnish with a parsley sprig.

Okra Curry

*A tasty vegetable curry
served over Basmati rice.*

12 or so	**Okras**
1	**Leek**
1	**Carrot**
2	**Potatoes**
4	**Garlic cloves, minced**
1 Tbl	**Curry**
1 tsp each	**Cumin seeds and dill**
2 tsp each	**Coriander and Tamari**
2 Tbl	**Cooking sherry**
	Hot filtered water to cover (approx. 1-2 cups)
	Dash of cayenne

1) Chop and slice all of the veggies
2) Put the vegetables into a pan with the garlic and spices (use your own taste with the spices), stir to coat the vegetables.
3) Cover the vegetables with filtered water. Bring the water to a boil, reduce to simmer and cover for 20 min. or until tender.

Serve with **Toasted Anise Rice** *(page 205) and* **Cucumbermint Raita** *(page 152).*

Serves 3

Tofu & Okra Sauté

1 Tbl	Tamari
1/2	Lemon, juiced
1 lg	Onion, peeled and chopped
4 lg	Garlic cloves, pressed
2 c	Okra, chopped
1	Bell pepper, sliced
1/2 blk	"Lite" firm tofu, cut in small cubes (approx. 8 oz.)
2 lg	Tomatoes, chopped
1 bunch	Green onions, chopped
1/2 tsp each	Cumin, ground coriander, oregano, cracked black pepper
1/2 to 1 c	Filtered water

1) In a large skillet, heat the tamari and lemon juice. Stir in the onions and garlic, then add the okra and peppers. Sauté for 5 minutes.
2) Add the tofu and the rest of the ingredients, cover with filtered water.
3) Simmer on low until the veggies are cooked, approximately one half hour, stir occasionally.

*Serve over **Yellow Rice** (page 204) or **Mustard Seed Quinoa** (page 205).*

Serves 2-4

Potato and Vegetable Curry

*For a beautiful Indian dinner serve this curry with **Cucumbermint Raita***, **Fig Chutney*** and **Toasted Anise Rice***.*

1 Tbl	Safflower oil
1/4 c	Filtered water
2½ Tbl	Master curry (page 156)
1	Onion, quartered and sliced
2	Garlic cloves, pressed
4	Red potatoes, cut in small cubes
2	Bell peppers, chopped
1/2 head	Cauliflower torn into flowers
1 sm	Eggplant, peeled, cut into cubes
1 lg	Carrot, sliced
2½ c	Filtered water
3	Roma tomatoes, cut into wedges

1) Heat the oil and filtered water in a large skillet, add the curry and stir until bubbly.
2) Add the onions, stir for 5 min., add the rest of the vegetables except the tomatoes.
3) Pour filtered water over the veggies, stir and cover for 20 minutes or so. When the vegetables are tender, stir in the tomatoes.

See pages 152, 153, and 205 respectively.

Serves 3-4

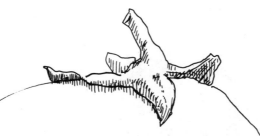

Eggplant Bean Threads

Woked vegetables seasoned with
sherry and ginger nestled in clear noodles.

1 pk	Bean thread noodles (about 4 oz.)
3 Tbl	Soy sauce
1 tsp	Honey
1/4 tsp	Ginger, skinned and grated
	Few drops toasted sesame oil
1	Eggplant
1 bunch	Green onions
3	Celery ribs
1	Tomato
3 Tbl	Cooking sherry
1 Tbl	Liquid aminos
1/2 c	Filtered water
1 c	Shelled green peas

1) Rinse and soak the bean thread noodles in warm filtered water (10 min.) until soft. Gently boil the noodles in a pot of filtered water until tender. This will only take a few minutes, drain.
2) Combine the next 4 ingredients and toss them into the noodles.
3) Peel and slice the eggplant into bite sized pieces, shred the onions diagonally, slice the celery, seed and chop the tomato.
4) Heat the sherry, liquid aminos and filtered water in a wok, then add the vegetables. Bring the liquids to a boil, then simmer until crisp tender. Stir in the noodles, coat them well with the veggies and serve warm.

Serves 2-4

Tempeh in Peanut Sauce

A tempeh "satay" in spicy peanut sauce.

8 oz	Tempeh
1 Tbl	Lemon juice
1 Tbl	Tamari
1/2	Onion, peeled
1/4 c	Filtered water
1 recipe	Tofu Thai Peanut Sauce (page 138)
	Bean threads or glass noodles, cooked al dente

1) Thinly slice the onion, chop the tempeh.
2) Marinate the 1st four ingredients for a few hours.
3) Place the water in a wok, heat up, then add the tempeh and marinade, cook for 15 minutes or until done.
4) Stir in the peanut sauce. Serve over the warm bean thread noodles.

Serve with **Thai Bright Salad** *(page 88).*

Serves 4

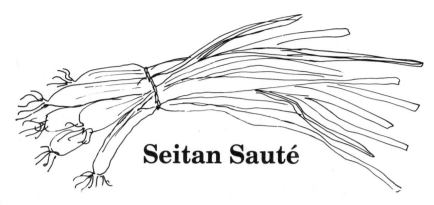

Seitan Sauté

Seasoned seitan* filets combine with woked vegetables, served rolled up in mu-shu pancakes.

1/2	Lime, juiced
1/2	Lemon juiced
1 Tbl	Tamari
2 Tbl	Filtered water (or more if you like it "juicy")
1/2" piece	Ginger, peeled and chopped
1 lg	Garlic clove, pressed
1	Jalapeño, seeded, minced (keep seeds in if you like spicy hot foods)
4	Zucchinis, chopped
1/2 lb	Mushrooms, sliced
1 bunch	Green onions, sliced
	Spiced Seitan, sliced (figure 2-3 slices per person)
	Mushu pancakes or tortillas
	Ornamental lettuces, fresh tomato wedges and cucumber spears

1) Heat up the juices, filtered water and tamari in a wok.
2) Add the ginger, garlic and jalapeño, stir and cover for a couple of minutes.
3) Add the vegetables, stir for another 5 minutes or so.
4) Add the seitan slices on top and let it steam until warmed. Place your pancakes on top to further steam if you want.
5) Garnish each dish or bowl with lettuces around the perimeter, fill each dish with woked veggies, place the seitan on top. Arrange the tomatoes and cucumber around the edges, serve with the warmed pancakes.

Serves 3-4

*See page 15.

Cabbage Noodles for 2

Woked shredded cabbage and oriental noodles
tossed in a seasoned sauce.

2	**Portions samen, ramen or soba noodles**
1/3 c	**Filtered water**
1/2 head	**Cabbage**
1	**Onion, peeled**
2	**Garlic cloves**
1/2 Tbl	**Mirin or cooking sherry**
1½ Tbl	**Tamari**
1 sm bunch	**Cilantro leaves**
	Dash of cayenne

1) Cook the noodles al dente, then drain.
2) Slice the vegetables thinly or shred them.
3) Heat the filtered water in a wok and then add the vegetables.
4) Cook on high heat for 4-5 minutes.
5) Add the last 4 items, stir, then put in the noodles and toss well.
6) Transfer to a serving platter.

*Serve with **Ginger Longbeans** (page 221).*

Serves 2-3

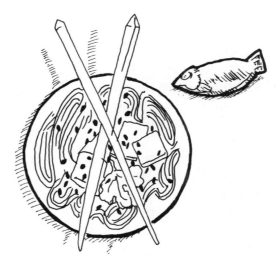

Tofu Marinade Over Daikon Shreds

A marvelous light meal with a Japanese flair.

Marinade Sauce:
1/4 c	Mirin (cooking sake)
1/4 c	Tamari
1/2 Tbl	Ginger root, skinned and minced
1 tsp	Honey

1 lb	"Lite" tofu, firm, sliced
1 c	Daikon, shredded
1/4 c	Yellow squash, shredded
1 c	Lettuce, shredded

1) Blend the sauce and pour it over the tofu slices, arrange them on a flat tray and refrigerate them overnight.
2) Heat gently or top broil the tofu. Or, use this crust: Mix together: 3 Tbl roasted ground sesame seeds and 2 Tbl flour (whole grain). Coat the tofu slices with flour and then sauté in liquid aminos until the tofu is browned on both sides.
3) Lay the tofu on top of the shredded veggies, serve.

Serves 2-4

Mushu Tofu

A delectable Chinese burrito, served with a spicy dipping sauce.
Serve the stir fry on a large platter along with the steamed pancakes.

1/2	**Block "Lite" tofu, firm**
1½ bunches	**Green onions**
3	**Zucchinis**
1	**Green pepper**
5	**Shiitake mushrooms**
1½ c	**Shredded woodears***
1 Tbl	**Canola oil or peanut oil**
2 Tbl	**Tamari**
1 Tbl	**Fresh ginger, skinned and grated**
1/4 tsp	**Toasted sesame oil**
1 tsp each	**Mirin and honey**
1 pk	**Mushu pancakes**
	Mushu sauce (see below)

1) Cut the tofu into thin strips. Mince the onions, then slice the zucchinis and the pepper into thin strips.
2) Soak the dried mushrooms and the woodears in filtered water until they are soft; discard the tough stems, then thinly slice the mushrooms and woodears.
3) Heat the oil and tamari in a wok, add the zucchinis and the peppers. Stir to coat. Then add the tofu, mushrooms and ginger, and after 3 minutes add the onions and woodears.
4) Pour the mirin and honey on top and stir quickly to coat evenly.
5) Serve the sauté rolled into hot pancakes, roll like a burrito with the ends folded. Serve with Mushu sauce if desired.

Mushu Sauce:

1/2 c	**Filtered water**	
1 tsp	**Arrowroot powder**	
1 Tbl each	**Miso and honey**	**Dash of cayenne and**
1/2 tsp each	**Minced ginger and garlic**	**Tamari to taste**

1) Mix the filtered water with arrowroot powder in a small saucepan using a whisk.
2) Heat gently, stirring until thickened. Add the rest of the ingredients and stir well.

Available in oriental markets, see page 17 for description.

Serves 4

Pineapple Soba Tempehtation

A sweet and sour tempeh stir fry with noodles.

1 (8 oz) pk	Tempeh
1 (8 oz) pk	Soba noodles
1	Red onion, peeled
2 lg	Bell peppers
1 c	Pineapple
2	Tomatoes, seeded
1 Tbl	Liquid aminos
1 tsp	Toasted sesame oil
	Filtered water as needed

Marinade

2 lg	Garlic cloves, pressed
1" piece	Fresh ginger, skinned and minced
2 tsp	Apple cider vinegar
	Dash of Cayenne
1 Tbl	Tamari

1) Chop the tempeh into cubes. Stir together the marinade, marinate the tempeh in the sauce overnight or for a few hours before meal preparation.
2) Cook the soba noodles in boiling water until al dente, strain and set aside.
3) Slice the onions, chop the peppers, pineapple and tomatoes.
4) Heat the liquid aminos in a wok, sauté the onion. Add the tempeh and a bit of filtered water, stir continuously.
5) Add the peppers and stir, then add the soba, and the rest of the veggies—turn off the heat when veggies are still crisp.
6) Stir in the sesame oil last—serve hot.

Serves 2-3

Thai Vegetable Sauté

Coconut and peanut flavor this exotic spicy sauté.

1 lg	Red bell pepper
(15 oz) can	Baby corn
10 med	Mushrooms
1 sm	Red onion, peeled
2 lg	Garlic cloves
1 Tbl	Liquid aminos
1	Lemon, juiced

Sauce:

1/2 c	Coconut milk
1/4 c	Peanut butter
1/2 Tbl	Tamari
dash of	Red chile flakes and cayenne
1/2" piece	Ginger, skinned and pressed through a garlic press
	Filtered water to thin

1) Slice the peppers, mushrooms and onion.
2) Press the garlic into the wok with the lemon juice and liquid aminos, sauté.
3) Add the rest of the veggies, stir until crisp-cooked.
4) Blend the sauce ingredients together, add filtered water if necessary, pour the sauce mixture over the vegetables, stir to coat.

*Serve with **Yellow Rice** (page 204), jasmine rice or couscous. If tofu or tempeh is desired, cube and marinate them in the coconut sauce for a few hours before adding them to the vegetable sauté.*

Serves 2-4

Wonton in Kombu Broth

These heavenly wontons are much too easy to eat,
be careful not to over cook.

1/2 lb	Firm "Lite" tofu, crumbled
2 lg	Garlic cloves, pressed
1" piece	Ginger, skinned and minced (fresh)
1/2 tsp	Lemon rind, grated
1 Tbl	Soy sauce
1 oz	Kombu (1 strip)
2 qts	Filtered water
1 bunch	Green onions, chopped
1 can	Water chestnuts (8 oz.)
1/2 tsp	Toasted sesame oil
	A couple of threads of saffron
1 pk	Wonton wrappers

1) Marinate the top 5 ingredients overnight.
2) Prepare the broth; put the washed kombu in the filtered water, bring to a boil and cook on medium heat for 1/2 hr.
3) Meanwhile make the wonton stuffing: put the green onions, filtered water chestnuts, oil and saffron into a blender or food processor, pulse chop them for several seconds. Add the marinated tofu and chop until a paste-like consistency forms.
4) Fill each wonton square with 1 heaping tsp. of filling, seal the edges with water. Fold the wonton into a triangle, twist its edges right over left and seal with more water.
5) Strain out the kombu from the broth, bring the broth back to a boil.
6) Add the wontons to the boiling broth. Cook for a couple of minutes then strain the wontons out. These cook very quickly, keep your eyes open!
7) Pour the broth into separate bowls, add a few wontons. Garnish with minced chives or cilantro.

Serves 4

Tofu in Vegetable Nests

*Hot tofu nestled in cool shredded vegetable nests—
a surprising combination.*

Nests:

2	**Carrots**
1/4	**Cabbage**
2	**Celery ribs**
1 Tbl	**Rice vinegar**
	Sesame oil, few drops

Tofu:

1/2 blk	**"Lite" firm tofu, diced**
1/4 c	**Peas**
2 Tbl	**Mirin**
1 Tbl	**Lemon juice**
1/2 Tbl	**Tamari**

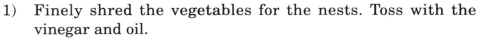

Buckwheat sprouts
Sunflower sprouts

1) Finely shred the vegetables for the nests. Toss with the vinegar and oil.
2) Sauté the tofu and peas in the liquids until hot and tender
3) Assemblage: press vegetables into nests in separate bowls, scoop the tofu into the nests. Surround each nest with long sprouts forming a ring.

Eat with chop sticks.

Serves 2

Pasta Exotica

This delicious pasta uses lotus roots, baby corn and tofu woked
with simmered greens. The sweet and spicy glaze works great
over fresh pastas. Add whatever vegetables or flowers you
wish and amaze your guests!

10 oz	"Savory Tofu"*
1 pk	Lotus root, boiled (approx. 5.2 oz)*
15 oz can	Baby corn
1 Tbl	Tamari
6 c	Shredded greens, packed (bokchoy, chard, etc.)
2 Tbl	Liquid aminos
	Red chili flakes and toasted sesame seeds, a couple of drops toasted sesame oil
1 lb	Pasta, fresh (try flavored kinds like red cajun tomato, jalapeño etc.)
1 recipe	Wok Glaze (page 141) (prepared ahead of time)
2	Tomatoes

1) Marinate the tofu slices, lotus and corn in tamari.
2) Cook the pasta al dente and keep it covered on the side.
3) Heat the wok, add the liquid aminos and tofu marinade mixture, stir, then cover for a minute.
4) Add the greens, cover to steam for a couple of minutes, then sprinkle the red chili flakes and sesame seeds on top, stir well to mix.
5) Pour the glaze into the vegetables in the wok, toss to coat evenly, add the toasted sesame oil—turn off the heat.
6) Put the pasta on a serving platter, mix in the woked vegetables and garnish with fresh tomato wedges.

Available in Natural Food Stores; a firm tofu that is marinated in tamari, soy sauce and spices.

Serves 3-4

Tempeh with Vegetables

Serves 2 hungry eaters.

1/4 c	Cooking sherry
2 Tbl	Lemon or lime juice
1 Tbl	Safflower oil
2 cloves	Garlic, minced
1 (8 oz) pk	Tempeh, cubed and steamed 10 minutes
1 lg	Green pepper, sliced
1/2 dz pk	Fresh oyster mushrooms
1/4 tsp	Roasted sesame oil
2 Tbl	Shoyu or tamari
1/4 c	Filtered water
1 lg	Tomato, cut into wedges
1 Tbl	Cilantro leaves, chopped

1) Heat the sherry, the oil and the lemon juice in a wok, add the garlic and tempeh. Stir on high heat until tempeh begins to brown.
2) Add the green pepper, stir for 2 minutes, add the rest of the ingredients (except for the tomato and the cilantro). Continue stirring until tender for 5 or so minutes.
3) Add the tomato, stir again and turn off the heat. Cover.
4) Toss in the cilantro before serving.

Serve with **Miso Sesame Rice** *(page 206), couscous or rice pilaf. Many tasty instant rice-like dishes are available for when you have no time.*

Serves 2-3

No Soba Soba

The parsnip resembles pasta in this all veggie, nicely spiced stirfry.

1 Tbl	Tamari
1/4 c	Lemon juice
2 Tbl	Mirin (cooking sake)
1 big	Parsnip, peeled and cut into 3" or 4" sections, then slice into thin pasta-like strips
1/4 head	Red cabbage, chopped
1/2	Eggplant, cubed and skinned
1" piece	Ginger, skinned and chopped
1/4 c	Filtered water
8	Shiitake mushrooms (fresh if possible)
1 bunch	Spinach, sliced
4	Garlic cloves, minced
1/2 lb	"Lite" firm tofu, cut into 1/2" cubes
Dash	Cayenne
	Sesame seeds as garnish

1) Put the first 3 liquids into a hot wok, add the parsnip "pasta", the cabbage and the eggplant, stir, then cover on med-hi heat, cook for 10 minutes, stir occasionally.

2) Meanwhile put the ginger in a blender with filtered water, blend, then add to the wok.

3) Add the rest of the ingredients, heat gently, stir to coat. Serve with rice.

Serves 2

Eggplant Nori Rolls

These are very easy to make, especially if you already have rice cooked.
Try different types of rice for variation.

3	Eggplant slices
1 Tbl	Filtered water
2 Tbl	Mirin (cooking sake)
	Squeeze of lemon
1 tsp	Minced fresh ginger
1 tsp	Tamari
1/4 tsp	Toasted sesame oil
	Gomasio or toasted sesame seeds
	Wasabi and tamari as condiments
1½ c	Quick Sushi Rice (page 206)
	Nori sheets

1) Cut each eggplant slice into 1/2" thick strips. (Makes 12 strips.)
2) Heat the water, add the mirin and lemon to a skillet or wok—add the minced fresh ginger, tamari and eggplant, stir while cooking (for a few minutes only), then turn off the heat.
3) Add the sesame oil, stir.
4) Take the nori sheet, lay a bed of rice over it covering 3/4 of the sheet. Lay 3 eggplant strips horizontally down the center of the nori sheet, sprinkle with gomasio, then carefully roll up the nori sheet using both hands. Seal the nori edges with filtered water.
5) Slice the nori rolls and arrange them on a platter. Serve with a dipping sauce of wasabi paste and tamari in individual bowls.

Makes 4 nori rolls.

DESSERTS

DESSERTS

Our passionate sweet tooth has inspired a great deal of experimentation to find healthy, nutritious, low calorie desserts that could truly satisfy.

Imagine eating chocolate mousse, cake and ice cream; all without dairy products, eggs, butter, refined sugar and flour. The recipes herein include refreshing and nonfattening mousses, puddings, parfaits, fruit sorbets and gels which are a perfect fulfillment to any meal.

Then there are a few cake, pie and torte recipes to intoxicate even the most spirited sweet tooth.

Go ahead and indulge in these enlightening desserts and taste a new level of sweetness in your life.

Fresh Fruit Desserts

Begin substituting fresh colorful juicy fruits as a dessert. It will quench your sweet tooth and is so much better for you, leaving you with a light (rather than stuffed) feeling after a wonderful meal.

Light and luscious dairyless desserts

Banana Ice Cream

The first all fruit ice cream we ever made,
one bite and we were addicted.

2   Bananas, frozen, chopped

1) Blend or puree the bananas in a food processor.
2) Stop and stir until thick and creamy, serve immediately.

Serves one

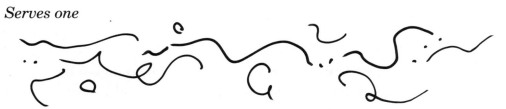

Cocoa Banana Ice Cream

1/2 lb   "Lite" soft tofu
2 c   Frozen bananas
1/4 c   Cocoa powder
1/4 c   Fructose or sweetener of choice

Blend in a food processor until creamy, refreeze 2 hours for extra icyness.

Serves 2

Chocolate Mousse

The silken tofu is the key to a light mousse.

1 pk	"Lite" silken soft tofu
1/3 c	Maple syrup or honey
2 Tbl	Cocoa powder
1 tsp	Vanilla extract
1 tsp	Peanut butter (optional)

Puree until smooth, refrigerate or freeze 2 hours before use.

Serves 3-4

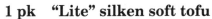

Fudgesicles

A great treat for kids!

Put chocolate mousse recipe into popsicle molds—freeze overnight or several hours.

Chocolate Mint Mousse

Follow chocolate mousse recipe and add:

1/4 tsp	Peppermint extract
	Garnish with a mint leaf

Serves 3-4

Raspberry Bavarian Mousse

Very easy to make and delicious, too!

1 pk	"Lite" silken tofu (10.5 oz)
1/4 c	Natural Raspberry syrup
3/4 c	Raspberries (frozen)
1/4 tsp	Almond extract
1/2 tsp	Vanilla extract

Puree until creamy, freeze for 1-2 hours before serving.

Serves 3-4

Strawberry Mousse

*To the above recipe substitute strawberries instead of raspberries,
use strawberry jam as a sweetener.*

Raspberry Cocoa Mousse

1 pk	"Lite" silken tofu
2 Tbl	Natural Raspberry syrup
2 Tbl	Cocoa powder
1 Tbl	Honey
1/4 c	Frozen raspberries

Puree all of the ingredients in a food processor, freeze the purée for
2 hours or refrigerate it overnight—garnish with fresh raspberries
or a mint leaf.

Serves 3-4

Fresh Fruit Ices

*Bananas, strawberries, peaches, apricots, or any frozen fruit creates
a refreshing dessert or afternoon treat.*

**Freeze berries or fruit of choice, put them into a
food processor or blender. Blend until smooth,
adding enough juice to blend. Serve immediately
or, freeze 1 hour to firm up your fresh fruit dessert
before serving it.**

Purple Passion

A cooling treat.

1/2 c	(4 oz.) "Lite" tofu, soft
1½ c	Frozen blueberries
2 Tbl	Honey or natural fruit syrup
	Few drops of peppermint oil or extract

Blend all until smooth—great after fiery spicy foods.

Serves 2-3

Piña Colada Sorbet

A tropical lo-cal sorbet.

2 c	Pineapple chunks
1	Banana
1/4 c	Pineapple coconut juice or orange juice

1) Freeze the pineapple overnight.
2) Blend or puree the frozen pineapple with the banana, adding
   the juice slowly. Stop and stir until it is all pureed—put into
   glasses or dessert cups and freeze for 1 hour before serving.

Serves 4

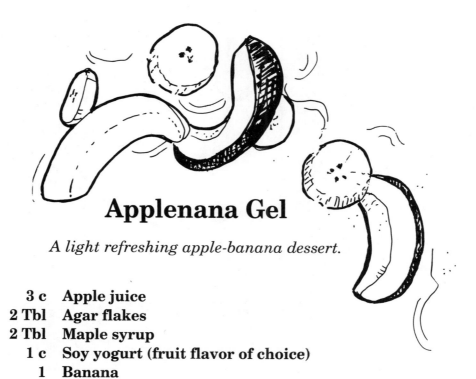

Applenana Gel

A light refreshing apple-banana dessert.

3 c	**Apple juice**
2 Tbl	**Agar flakes**
2 Tbl	**Maple syrup**
1 c	**Soy yogurt (fruit flavor of choice)**
1	**Banana**
1	**Anna apple**
	Sprinkle of clove and cinnamon

1) Whisk the agar into 1/2 cup of apple juice.
2) Heat the rest of the apple juice (including the agar mixture) in a small saucepan until boiling. Reduce the heat, stir in the spices and syrup, continue cooking on low heat for 3-5 minutes. When cool, stir in the soy yogurt.
3) Slice the fruit and put the fruit inside a 4-cup mold.
4) Pour the cooled juice on top—chill in the freezer for 2 hours, or until firm.

Serves 4

Fresh Fruit Ring

A beautiful low-cal fresh fruit mold.

2	Baskets of sweet fresh strawberries, sliced
2	Peaches, sliced
6 oz	Fresh fruit smoothie (or 1¾ cup juice blended with 2 very ripe or frozen bananas)
1/8 c	Coconut shredded
1½ tsp	Agar
1/2 c	Filtered water

1) Mix the filtered water and agar together. Bring to a boil with some of the juice—stir and simmer.
2) Put the sliced fruit into a bowl—pour in the rest of the juice and agar—mix thoroughly.
3) Pour into a decorative ring mold and chill in the freezer for 1½ hours, then serve (or refrigerate for several hours). Invert onto a pretty glass plate, decorate with flowers or sliced fruit.

Serves 4

Fruity Vanilla Parfait

Layer one, red:

1 c	Frozen fruit of choice (raspberries, strawberries)
2 Tbl	Natural fruit syrup
1/4 c	Low fat soy yogurt (berry flavored)

Layer two, white, yellow or green:

1 c	Fresh frozen fruit of choice (kiwis, bananas, peaches or apricots)
1/2 c	Low fat soy yogurt (lemon or mango)
1 tsp	Vanilla extract
1 Tbl	Honey or fruit syrup

Topping:

**Fruit soy yogurt drizzled with fruit
syrup and fresh fruit spears or berries.**

1) Blend the 1st group, spoon the blended mixture into small parfait glasses or champagne flutes. Put in a freezer for 1-2 hours.
2) Blend the 2nd group and spoon it on top. Chill in the freezer for 2 hours.
3) Let thaw for 1/2 hour before serving. Add topping.

Makes 3-4 servings

Amazake Carob Pudding

*A naturally sweetened cultured rice drink that makes a quick
and easy rice pudding.*

16 oz   **Amazake**
1 Tbl   **Carob powder**
1 Tbl   **Arrowroot powder and filtered water to thin**
            Toasted almond slivers for garnish
            Honey, if desired

1)   Gently heat the amazake in a small pan.
2)   Mix the arrowroot with the filtered water, add the mixture to
     the amazake.
3)   Whisk in the carob, heat until thick. Pour into dessert glasses
     or wine glasses, chill a few hours before serving. Top with the
     almond slivers.

Serves 3

Tofu Flan

A silky custard with hints of orange and lemon, baked in a caramelized syrup. It is best served chilled, complementary to spicy foods.

Caramel:

1/2 c	**Fructose**
3 Tbl	**Filtered water**
1/2 tsp	**Vanilla extract**
1/4 tsp	**Almond extract**

Custard:

30 oz	**Silken "Lite" tofu (2 packs)**
1 tsp	**Vanilla extract**
1 Tbl	**Orange liqueur (or 1 tsp extract)**
1 tsp	**Lemon peel, grated**
1/2 c	**Fresh squeezed orange juice**
2 tsp	**Agar flakes**

1) Preheat oven to 350°.
2) Combine the caramel ingredients in a small heavy saucepan, stir and cook over medium heat until it becomes amber colored, no more than 5 minutes total.
3) Pour a spoonful of the caramel into each dry muffin tin and set aside.
4) Puree the custard ingredients (except for the O.J. and the agar) in a food processor. Stir the agar into the O.J. and bring them to a boil for one minute in a small saucepan. Stir this into the custard and pour the custard mixture into the muffin tin.
5) Place the muffin tin into a larger pan and fill the outer pan with 1" depth of water (so the muffin tin "floats" in the water).
6) Bake for 30 minutes, cool for 2 hours before serving. Before inverting the flan, loosen it with a knife along the perimeter of the muffin tin, then invert them on a plate. Remove the muffin tin and serve!

Serves 6

Silken Orange Carrot Pie

A light delicious pie with a gorgeous orange color and the fragrance of spicy orange blossoms.

2 c	Carrots, pureed
3/4 c	Fresh orange juice
2 Tbl	Agar flakes
1 Tbl	Arrowroot powder
10.5 oz pk	Silken "Lite" tofu
1 tsp	Orange rind, grated
1/4 tsp	Cardamom, fresh ground
dash of each	Cinnamon and clove powder
1 recipe	Granola Pie Crust (page 296)

1) Chop and cook the carrots until soft—then puree.
2) Mix the O.J. with the agar and arrowroot, bring them to a boil in a small saucepan. Stir for 1 minute until thick, then set aside.
3) Add the tofu, spices and O.J. mixture to the carrots, and puree them all in a food processor.
4) Pour the puree into a pie crust, chill for several hours or overnight until set.

Serve with **Sauce of Angels** *(page 111) or vanilla soy ice cream if desired.*

Serves 6-8

Cocoa Berry Cream Pie

A luscious low fat dessert that is best served quite chilled. Blueberries enliven this dairyless cocoa pie.

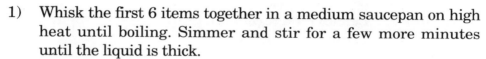

2 c	"Lite" cocoa soy milk
1/4 c	Agar flakes
1 tsp	Vanilla extract
1 Tbl	Carob powder
3 Tbl	Maple syrup
1 Tbl	Arrowroot powder
1½ c	Blueberries (fresh or frozen)

1) Whisk the first 6 items together in a medium saucepan on high heat until boiling. Simmer and stir for a few more minutes until the liquid is thick.

2) Stir in the blueberries and pour the mixture into the **Almondine Crust** (below). Refrigerate until firm, for at least 2-4 hours before serving.

Almondine Crust

A wonderful crust of soaked almonds.

1 c	Almonds (soaked in filtered water overnight, minimum 10 hrs.)
1/4 c	Raisins
3 Tbl	Wholewheat pastry flour
1 Tbl	Peanut butter
dash	Cinnamon

1) Drain the almonds and grind all of the ingredients together in a food processor.

2) Press the ground mixture into a non-stick pie pan and bake the crust in a preheated oven at 400° for 15 minutes. Fill with the **Cocoa Berry Cream Pie** filling and then chill until firm.

Serves 6-8

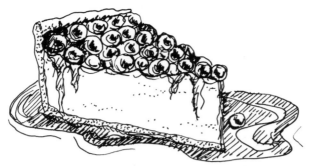

Blueberry Almondine "Cheesecake"

*A luscious non-dairy, tofu pie with grated lemon peel and fresh blueberries, top it with the **Blueberry Glaze** (next page).*

10.5 oz	"Lite" silken soft tofu
8.5 oz	"Lite" vanilla soy milk (1½ cups)
1/4 c	Agar flakes
2 Tbl	Honey
1/4 tsp	Almond extract
1/2 tsp	Lemon rind (organic), grated
1¼ c	Fresh blueberries

1) Blend all of the ingredients except for the berries in a food processor or a blender until silky.

2) Transfer to a medium pot and bring to rolling boil (on medium-hi heat), stirring constantly with a whisk. Set aside to cool down a bit.

3) Pour the "cheesecake" into the **Almond Crust** (below). Let the "cheesecake" sit for a few minutes, then put the blueberries on top and refrigerate.

Almond Crust

1 c	Soaked almonds
1/4 c	Raisins
1/2 Tbl	Peanut butter
1/4 c	Oatbran
1/4 tsp	Almond extract

Grind all of the ingredients, press the ground mixture into a shallow quiche dish. Bake for 15 minutes at 375° in a preheated oven.

Serves 6

Blueberry Glaze

*Use to top "cheesecakes",
or fruity / soy based ice creams.*

1 c	**Blueberries**
1 Tbl	**Kuzu (wild Japanese arrowroot)**
2 Tbl	**Filtered water**
1 c	**Fruit juice (apple, raspberry, etc.)**
1/2 tsp	**Almond extract**

1) Wash the berries, set them aside.
2) Dissolve the kuzu in the filtered water, put the liquid into a small pan with the juice. Bring them to a boil, stirring constantly. Turn to low heat and cook until the mixture thickens, just a couple minutes. Stir in the extract.
3) Stir in the berries, simmer for a few more minutes. Serve hot over "cheesecake".

Makes 1¼ cups

Persimmon Ice Creme Pie

A divinely colored no-bake cheesecake.

16 oz	Silken "Lite" tofu
3 lg	Persimmons, ripe
1/2 tsp	Vanilla
1 tsp packed	Grated lemon peel
1/3 c	Honey or date paste

1) Put the tofu and honey in a food processor and blend them until smooth.
2) Mash the persimmons and then add the other ingredients, puree them all together.
3) Pour the puree into a pie shell—we suggest the **Granola Pie Crust** below.
4) Freeze the **Persimmon Ice Creme Pie** for several hours, until set.

Let thaw 1½ hours before serving.

Serves 6

Granola Pie Crust

A "no-bake" pie crust.

2 c	Fat-free granola, (finely ground in a blender)
1½ Tbl	Raw tahini
1/8 c	Barley malt or rice syrup
2-3 Tbl	Cold filtered water

Stir all of the ingredients together with a fork and press the mixture into a fluted dish or pie pan. Or, you may roll out the crust between 2 sheets of wax paper, then press it into the pie dish.

Makes 1 pie crust

Pear Custard Cream Pie

*A dairyless custard pudding makes a great base
for fresh sliced ripe pears.*

5-6	**Ripe pears**
1	**Lemon , juiced**
2 tsp	**Fructose**
2 Tbl	**Arrowroot powder or Kuzu**
1 Tbl	**Agar**
1½ c	**Creamy fat-free ("Lite" is o.k.) soy milk**
1	**Pastry crust, pre-baked (page 300)**
2 Tbl	**Dark chocolate (or carob) chips, melted, thin with 1 Tbl filtered water**

1) Skin, core and slice the pears. Put them into a bowl and toss them with the lemon juice and fructose.

2) Mix the arrowroot and agar with 1/4 cup of the soy milk until smooth. Transfer to a heavy pot, adding the rest of the soy milk, heat on medium. Stir until the mixture thickens. Mix 1/2 of the pears into the custard.

3) Grate the peel from the lemon, stir into the custard. Melt the chocolate.

4) Now assemble in the pastry crust: put the custard on the bottom, arrange the pears on top of the custard, then drizzle the chocolate fancifully, chill for several hours before serving.

Serves 6

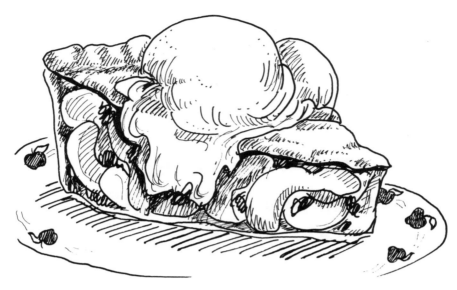

Apple Pie

A hearty and spicy pie, delicious with vanilla soy ice cream or
Banana Ice Cream *(page 283).*

3 lg	Apples, skinned, cored, sliced thin
2 Tbl	Wholewheat pastry flour
1/2	Lemon, juiced
1/4 c	Raisins, soaked (monukahs are best)
2 Tbl	Maple syrup
1/8 tsp	Fresh grated nutmeg
1 tsp	Cinnamon
1/4 c	Granola (maple is good)
1	Pastry crust (page 300)

1) Prepare the apples, pre-bake the pie shell (6 min. at 375°).
2) Squeeze the lemon over the apples in a medium size bowl, toss with the rest of the ingredients.
3) Grind the granola in a blender. Fill the pie crust with the apples. Sprinkle on the granola and bake until brown—approx. 25-30 min. at 350°.

Serves 6

Tropical Rice Pudding

A sweet and chewy rice delight.

2 c	Filtered water
1 c	Sweet brown rice, rinsed
2 c	Vanilla "Lite" soy milk
1 c	Pineapple chunks
1/4 c	Coconut, shredded, lightly toasted
1/4 c	Dried papaya, diced
2 Tbl	Egg replacer beaten stiff with 8 Tbl filtered water
1 Tbl	Arrowroot powder
1	Banana, sliced
1 tsp	Rum extract (optional)
1 Tbl	Apple concentrate or sweetener of choice

1) Bring the filtered water to a near boil, stir in the rice, cover, turn to simmer and cook for 35 minutes, turn off the heat.

2) Add the soy milk and the fruits, fold in the remaining ingredients, put the mixture into a non-stick baking dish. Bake at 350° for 30-40 minutes.

Serves 4-6

Zucchini Bread Pudding

Fresh ginger and cinnamon seasons the versatile zucchini,
a sweet treat.

3 c	Wholewheat raisin bread, cubed and gently toasted
2 c	Zucchini, coarsely chopped
1/3 c	Currants or raisins
2 c	"Lite" soy milk
1½ Tbl	Egg replacer
1 Tbl	Arrowroot
2 tsp	Vanilla extract
1 tsp each	Cinnamon and fresh ginger, skinned and minced
1/3 c	Fructose (or 1/4 cup honey)
dash of	Clove and nutmeg

1) Toss the first 3 items in a large bowl.
2) Blend the soy milk with the rest of the goodies. Pour the blended mixture over the bread mixture, toss them together gently and pour them into a non-stick baking dish. Bake for 1 hour at 375°.

Serves 4

Pastry Crust

1/3 c	Soy margarine
1½ c	Wholewheat pastry flour
1/2	Lemon, juiced (1 Tbl)
1/3 c	Walnuts, finely ground

1) Cut in the soy margarine with the rest of the ingredients—using a fork (or pulse chop in a food processor just until thick). Add 1-2 Tbl of filtered ice water, as needed.
2) Press the dough evenly into a non-stick pie pan—forming a crust, work from the center of the pan out. Pre-bake at 375° for 5 minutes, let cool then fill with fruit or filling of choice.

Makes 1 pie crust

Brandy Orange Cake

*A moist and luscious no oil, no egg cake layered with a light **Tofu Orange Creme Frosting** (see next page).*

1 tsp	**Orange liqueur or extract**
2 Tbl	**Brandy**
2 med	**Oranges**
2 Tbl	**Egg replacer mixed with**
1/3 c	**Soy yogurt**
1/2 c	**Honey**
1 tsp	**Vanilla**
3 Tbl	**Turbinado or date sugar**
1½ c	**Wholewheat pastry flour**
2 tsp	**Baking soda**
2 tsp	**Baking powder**
1 recipe	**Tofu Orange Creme Frosting (page 302)**

1) Skin, seed and chop the oranges. Put them into a small saucepan with the liqueur or orange extract, then simmer covered for a few minutes.
2) Meanwhile beat the egg replacer with the soy yogurt until thick and foamy, then add the rest of the wet ingredients.
3) Sift the dry items together then fold them into the wet ingredients, add the oranges (strain slightly first).
4) Spoon into a non-stick round casserole dish (9" diameter), bake at 375° for 40 minutes, or until your knife comes out clean.
5) Let cool, then turn over the casserole dish to remove the cake. Slice the cake into 2 cakes (horizontally) and frost in between and on top, refrigerate.

Garnish with thinly sliced oranges and raspberries.

Serves 4-6

Tofu Orange Creme Frosting

Heavenly frosting, chill to set.

5 oz	Silken "Lite" tofu
2 Tbl	Honey
2 Tbl	Frozen O.J. concentrate
dash of	Cinnamon and vanilla extract

1) Blend all of the ingredients until smooth.
2) Refrigerate the frosting.

Pineapple Walnut Upside Down Cake

No oil in this cake, yet so moist and delicious!

5	Pineapple rings
1 Tbl	Egg replacer mixed with 4 Tbl filtered water
1½ c	Fructose or natural sweetener
2 c	Wholewheat pastry flour
2 tsp	Baking powder
1 tsp	Vanilla
1 c	Walnuts, coarsely chopped
1 c	Pineapple, crushed

1) Arrange the pineapple slices in a circle, on the bottom of a non-stick bundt pan or cake pan of choice.
2) Blend the egg replacer, add the fructose, flour, baking powder and vanilla.
3) Fold in the walnuts and the crushed pineapple, pour the mixture into the cake pan and bake at 350° for 40-45 minutes.
4) To remove the cake invert the pan when cool.

*Serve with **Sauce of Angels** (page 111) or **Tofu Orange Creme Frosting** (above).*

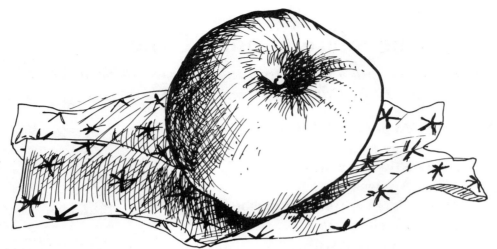

Apple Pecan Cake

A moist cake, not too sweet, great with vanilla soy ice cream.

1½ c	**Flour—unbleached**
1/2 c	**Bran**
1 tsp	**Baking powder**
1/2 tsp	**Soda**
1/2 tsp	**Cinnamon**
2 Tbl	**Poppy seeds**
2	**Apples, peeled and cored**
3/4 c	**Pecans—toasted**
1/2 c	**Soy yogurt low-fat (plain or flavored)**
2 Tbl	**Egg replacer mixed with 4 Tbl filtered water**
1/2 c	**Honey or apple concentrate**
1 tsp	**Vanilla**

1) Blend all of the dry ingredients (1st six items).
2) Chop the apples, chop the pecans.
3) Blend all of the wet ingredients (last 4 items).
4) Fold all of the ingredients together, put them into a non-stick small bundt pan or mold. (Putting a few half pecans in a circle on the bottom of the pan first). Bake for 30-40 minutes at 350°. To remove the cake invert the pan before serving.

Serves 4-6

Chocolate Almond Cake

*This is lightly sweet with a nice nutty texture. Serve with soy ice cream or with the **Carob Frosting** listed below.*

1/2 c	Almonds (lightly toasted)
1 Tbl	Egg replacer
4 Tbl	Filtered water
1/2 c	Applesauce
1/4 c	Dates, pitted and mashed
1/2 c	Maple syrup
1 tsp each	Vanilla and almond extract
1/3 c	"Lite" soy milk
6 Tbl	Cocoa powder
1¼ c	Unbleached flour
2 tsp	Baking powder

1) Grind the almonds finely in a nut mill, then put them into a medium mixing bowl. Preheat the oven at 375°.

2) Put the egg replacer and the filtered water into a food processor and puree them until fluffy. Add the applesauce, dates, maple syrup, and extracts. Then blend them well.

3) Sift the dry ingredients together into the bowl with the almonds. Stir in the wet mixture.

4) Use a non-stick round cake pan, pour in the batter and bake for 35 minutes at 375°.

Serves 4-6

Carob Frosting

A thick and creamy frosting that is low-fat and high in nutrition.

1 pk	Silken "Lite" tofu (10.5 oz.)
2 Tbl	Carob powder
2 Tbl	Honey
1/2	Lemon peel, grated
1 Tbl	Protein powder

Blend all of the ingredients until creamy, chill before using.

Peanut Butter Cake with Cocoa Frosting

*A moist cake. This will satisfy those
peanut butter and chocolate
sweet tooths.*

Cake:

1¼ c	Wholewheat pastry flour
1 tsp	Baking powder
1/4 tsp	Baking soda
1/2 pack	Silken "Lite" tofu
1/4 c	Safflower oil
2/3 c	Fructose or sucanat
1/3 c	Peanut butter
1/2 Tbl	Vanilla
1/3 c	Filtered water blended with
1 Tbl	Postum or pero
1/3 c	"Lite" soy milk

Cocoa Frosting:

2 Tbl	Vanilla or chocolate low-fat soy milk
1 c	Silken "Lite" tofu
3 Tbl	Cocoa powder
2 Tbl	Protein powder
1 tsp	Vanilla
1/3 c	Fructose or sucanat
1 Tbl	Peanut butter

1) Sift the flour, baking powder and baking soda together.
2) Blend the remaining wet ingredients separately. Stir the wet and dry mixtures together.
3) Pour the cake batter into a non-stick cake pan and bake for 35 min. at 375°.
4) Blend the frosting ingredients together (refrigerate to set) frost the cake when frosting is cool.

Serves 12

Brownies

A delicious "low-fat" brownie. Frost with the
Cocoa Frosting *on page 305 for an extra treat.*

1½ Tbl	Egg replacer mixed with 4 Tbl filtered water
1 tsp	Vanilla
1/2 c	Date paste*
1/2 c	Applesauce
1/3 c	Cocoa or carob powder
1/3 c	Oat flakes
1/3 c	Maple syrup
3/4 c	Wholewheat pastry flour
1 tsp	Cinnamon
1 c	Walnuts, chopped, lightly toasted

1) Beat the egg replacer and the vanilla in a food processor. Pulse chop in the dates and the applesauce.
2) Add the remaining ingredients (except the nuts), and blend together.
3) Stir in the nuts, put the mixture into a 7" square non-stick baking pan and bake 25 minutes at 350°.

Date paste is simply mashed pitted dates. You can sometimes find it in natural food co-ops. Use moist dates like barhi or medjool.

Serves 12

Open Sesame Balls

Makes 18 sweet candies.

1/2 c   **Sesame tahini**
1/4 c   **Date pieces**
1 Tbl   **Carob powder**
2 Tbl   **Honey**
2 Tbl   **Sesame seeds**
2 Tbl   **Coconut, shredded**

1) Blend the first 5 goodies together in a food processor. Form the blended mixture into balls, about 1" in diameter.
2) Roll the balls in the shredded coconut and then refrigerate them.

Makes 18 balls

Trailblazers

These are protein packed balls, perfect for hiking or other all day adventures.

1 c   **Granola**
1/4 c   **Pumpkin seeds**
1/4 c   **Sun seeds**
1/4 c   **Almonds**
2 Tbl   **Flax seeds**
1/4 c   **Peanut butter or tahini**
1/4 c   **Barley malt syrup***
2 Tbl   **Vegetable protein powder**
1/4 c   **Bee pollen**

1) Grind the granola and the nuts until they are finely ground.
2) Stir in the peanut butter, syrup, protein powder and the bee pollen.
3) Oil your hands and roll the mixture into about 1" in diameter balls—then chill.

Add more honey, if necessary, to bind it all together. You can add dates or raisins too. Yum yum!

Bibliography

Books

Robbins, John. *Diet for a New America.* Stillpoint Publishing, 1987.

Jones, Alex. *Seven Mansions of Color.* DeVorss & Co., 1982.

Kowalchik-Hylton, Claire and William H. *Rodele's Illustrated Encyclopaedia of Herbs.* Rodele Press 1987.

Lau, Benjamin. *Garlic for Health.* 1988.

Erasmus, Udo. *Fats & Oils.* Alive Books, 1986.

Dextreit-Abehsera, Raymond-Michel. *Our Earth Our Cure.* Swan House Publishing Co., 1974.

Kirchmann, John D. *Nutrition Search, Inc. Nutrition Almanac.* McGraw-Hill Book Co., 1975.

Walker, N.W., D. Sci. *Raw Vegetable Juices.* A Pyramid Book, 1976.

Cousens, Gabriel, M.D. *Spiritual Nutrition and the Rainbow Diet.* Cassandra Press, 1986.

Kulvunkas, Victor. *Survival into the 21st Century.* 21st Century Publications, 1975.

Hill, Ray. *Propolis.* Thorsons Publishing, Ltd., 1977.

Wigmore, Anne. *Wheatgrass.* Avery Publishing Group, Inc., 1985.

Burroughs, Stanley. *The Master Cleanser.* Stanley Burroughs, 1976.

References

[1] Erasmus, Udo. *Fats & Oils*. Alive Books, 1986.

[2] Ibid.

[3] Kowalchik-Hylton, Claire and William H. *Rodele's Illustrated Encyclopaedia of Herbs*. Rodele Press 1987.

[4] Walker, N.W., D.Sci. *Raw Vegetable Juices*. Pyramid Books, 1976.

[5] Cousens, Gabriel. *Spiritual Nutrition and the Rainbow Diet*. Cassandra Press, 1986.

[6] Jones, Alex. *Seven Mansions of Color*. DeVorss & Company, 1982.

Alphabetical Index